# THE DYNAMICS OF MEDIEVAL ICELAND

*The Dynamics of Medieval*

# ICELAND

❖   ❖   ❖   ❖   ❖   ❖   ❖   ❖   ❖

*Political Economy & Literature*

E. PAUL DURRENBERGER

UNIVERSITY OF IOWA PRESS ᛩ IOWA CITY

University of Iowa Press, Iowa City 52242

Copyright © 1992 by the University of Iowa Press

Printed in the United States of America

Design by Richard Hendel

Printed on acid-free paper

96  95  94  93  92  C

5  4  3  2  1


Library of Congress Cataloging-in-Publication Data

Durrenberger, E. Paul, 1943–

The dynamics of medieval Iceland: political economy and

literature/by E. Paul Durrenberger.

p.  cm.

Includes bibliographical references and index.

ISBN 0-87745-388-8 (cloth)

1. Iceland—Politics and government.  2. Sagas—History and

criticism.  I. Title.

DL355.D87  1992

949.12—dc20                                            92-12335

CIP

FOR DOROTHY

# CONTENTS

Preface, ix

Acknowledgments, xiii

Chapter One. Introduction, 1

Chapter Two. Production, 25

Chapter Three. Chiefly Consumption, 41

Chapter Four. Politics, 52

Chapter Five. Exchange, 65

Chapter Six. Kinship, Church, and King, 75

Chapter Seven. Ideology, 79

Chapter Eight. Conclusions, 99

References Cited, 109

Index, 119

# PREFACE

The purpose of this book is to bring anthropological perspectives to bear on the study of medieval Iceland and to bring medieval Iceland into the purview of anthropology.

As witness to four hundred years of social, economic, and political change, medieval Iceland has left us a rich manuscript tradition which provides access not only to a single past but to processes of continuous change. Although Kirsten Hastrup (1985) has written from one anthropological perspective, she has not developed an analysis of the political economy of medieval Iceland or the connections between it and its cultural artifacts, the central theme of this work. One of the chief subjects of anthropology is the relationships among culture, thought, and material conditions as dimensions of such processes. Like other societies, medieval Iceland is best understood in terms of comparison with others.

Since most anthropologists, specialized in their own geographic and temporal areas, are not familiar with the Icelandic literary tradition, I have illustrated my arguments with examples. Most saga scholars are unfamiliar with the discipline of anthropology. Even those who have broken with tradition and gone in the direction of social and legal history show but scant awareness of the literature, arguments, and findings of anthropology. While this book may not expand their knowledge of the Icelandic tradition, it may expand their ideas of how to think about it.

The two most important facts about the medieval Icelandic social order are that it was stratified and that there was no state. For a period of some four hundred years between its Norse settlement and its incorporation into the kingdom of Norway in 1264, Iceland had to contend with the problem of how to maintain order and claims to property, upon which the system of extraction rested, without resorting to state institutions such as those in Norway, from which the chieftains had fled. That the Icelanders managed to do so for nearly four hundred years is a testimony to their tenacity. That they failed is a consequence of the inherent contradictions of the system they had brought with them from Norway and tried to perpetuate in Iceland.

People's claims to resources depended on their ability to defend them from others rather than on law or state institutions. Performative and aesthetic dimensions of resulting altercations were central to the maintenance of order. Reputation was important. Reputations were made and broken by the stories people told. Stories, sagas, were a central part of the system itself, and at least some of these have come down to us.

Our task is to situate the sagas in the political context of the period of their production, the thirteenth-century period of strife known as the Sturlung age. Unfortunately, we do not know who wrote the sagas, and it is implausible that any amount of debate will reveal the facts of their composition, though Sverrir Tómasson's arguments (1977) for an authorship beyond the cloister are convincing. What we do know of the sagas is that they are thirteenth-century interpretations of tenth- and eleventh-century life in Iceland. One question to pose is what such interpretations can tell us of the social and political realities of either period.

The social order of medieval Iceland contained within it a dynamism that inexorably led to the discord of the Sturlung period. People of the time interpreted their experiences with the cultural categories they had, and from their interpretations produced, among other artifacts, the family sagas and the contemporary Sturlung sagas. People revalued concepts such as honor, reciprocity, and law, all of which the political maneuvering of the age reduced in salience. Medieval Icelanders' valuations and revaluations informed not only their writing about contemporary events and the past, but their actions as well. In the sagas, Gabrielle Spiegel's (1990) sense of social agency, men and women struggling, is palpable.

All of the translations here are mine except those attributed and those from *Bandamanna Saga*, which Jonathan Wilcox and I did together. The chapter references to the family sagas are standard in all editions. I have translated selected passages from the edition edited by Bragi Halldórsson, Jón Torfason, Sverrir Tómasson, and Örnólfur Thorsson and published by Svart Á Hvítu in 1987. The chapter references for the contemporary Sturlunga sagas follow the system of the edition edited by Jón Jóhannesson, Magnús Finnbogason, and Kristján Eldjárn published in 1946 and Julia McGrew and R. George Thomas in their 1970 and 1974 translations. I have taken the text from the Svart Á Hvítu edition edited by Örnólfur Thorsson, published in 1988. For *Grágás* I have followed the text and chapter references of Vilhjálmur Finsen's 1852 edition, the same one Andrew Dennis et al. (1980) used.

I have retained Icelandic letters. The main differences between the Icelandic and modern English alphabets are the Icelandic "Þ, þ" (like the English "th" of "thing") and the Icelandic "Ð, ð" (like the English "th" of "this").

# ACKNOWLEDGMENTS

I first went to Iceland in 1981. Many people have shared with me their knowledge and enthusiasm for matters Icelandic through conversation, collaboration, and friendship. They include Dorothy Durrenberger, Þórólfur Þórlindsson, Gísli Pálsson, Guðný Guðbjörnsdóttir, Ástáður Eysteinsson, Jón Haukur Ingimundarson, Níels Einarsson, Hjörleifur Jónsson, Halldór Guðnason, Ástríður Guðný Daníelsdóttir, Ástríður Guðmundsdóttir, Daníel Guðmundsson, Jonathan Wilcox, Thomas McGovern, Bob Quinlan, and Julie Gurdin. Hjörleifur Jónsson read the manuscript, checked the translations, and provided useful comments. Jonathan Wilcox also read the manuscript and offered helpful comments. Readers should not blame any of these people for parts of the book they do not like.

Some material in this work first appeared as "Icelandic Sagas: A Window on a Medieval World" in the April 1992 issue of *The World & I* and is reprinted with permission from *The World & I* magazine, a publication of the Washington Times Corporation. Some material appeared in "Law and Literature in Medieval Iceland" in *Ethnos* 57 (1992), and is used with permission. Other material has appeared previously in other forms and is used here with permission. This material includes the following.

1985    Sagas, totems, and history. *Samfélagstíðindi* 5: 51–80.
1988a   Stratification without a state: The collapse of the Icelandic Commonwealth. *Ethnos* 53: 239–265.
1988b   Chiefly consumption in Commonwealth Iceland. *Northern Studies* 25: 108–120.
1990a   Production in medieval Iceland. *Acta Archaeologica* 61: 14–21. The Norse of the North Atlantic, ed. Gerald F. Bigelow.
1990b   Text and transactions in Commonwealth Iceland. *Ethnos* 55: 74–91.

A Faculty Development Leave from the University of Iowa and an appointment at Iowa's Center for Advanced Studies provided support for my work on this book. I thank Jay Semel, director of the Center, and Lorna Olson and the staff for their support.

# THE DYNAMICS OF
# MEDIEVAL ICELAND

# 1. INTRODUCTION

One summer in the thirteenth century, an Icelandic chieftain named Gissur, the son of Þorvaldur, got a letter from Hákon, the king of Norway. He was either to return Snorri, son of Sturla, to Norway or to kill him. Snorri had offended the king by leaving Norway without his permission. Gissur knew that Snorri, the most powerful chieftain in Iceland at that time, would not return to Norway, so with seventy of his followers and a larger force in reserve he rode to Snorri's establishment and broke into the house where he was sleeping. Snorri escaped. A neighboring priest denied knowledge of Snorri's whereabouts until Gissur told him that they had come to make an agreement with Snorri. When the priest admitted that Snorri was in the cellar, five of Gissur's men went below and three of them stabbed Snorri to death.

Thus died one of Iceland's greatest authors. Snorri was not only a shrewd political maneuverer, an astute and cunning arranger of marriages and alliances, a keeper of Iceland's laws, and a past master at the accumulation of wealth and power, he was also the writer of a handbook of poetry, a history of the kings of Norway, and possibly of the saga of his ancestor Egill Skalla-Grímur's son, one of Iceland's most famous warrior-poets. When Snorri was killed late in the year 1241, he was probably the most powerful and richest man in Iceland.

Such a death could not go unavenged. Snorri's son Órækja and brother's son, Sturla Þórður's son, gathered their forces and attacked Gissur's followers, who were occupying Snorri's house. They climbed the walls Snorri had built, then Órækja went into the main hall and ordered the men to surrender and lay down their arms. Later they killed Kolbeinn, the leader of that group.

I

With about five hundred men Snorri's avengers rode toward Gissur's house, where he was holding a feast on the eighth day of Christmas. When Gissur heard the news, he and his men fled to the bishopric at Skálholt. When the bishop offered to try to effect a reconciliation, Órækja agreed, but Gissur wanted to submit the case to the king of Norway in person. The bishop returned to Gissur and advised him that Órækja was likely to attack. He armed his clerics and offered to help Gissur with his defense.

Órækja's men attacked, and the battle raged. The bishop, clad in full vestments, his miter on his head, crozier in one hand, and a Bible and candle in the other, leapt up on the house beams and began to excommunicate Órækja and his followers. Órækja agreed to reconciliation; after much commotion, the battle was stopped. Gissur agreed to let the bishop decide the case. When Gissur and Órækja shook hands and swore on the cross, the bishop freed the men from excommunication and offered them food.

Gissur then went to Norway and spent three years with the king, who assigned to him the whole northern quarter of Iceland. When he returned to Iceland and read the king's letter publicly, he was accepted as chieftain of the north.

Another group attacked Gissur in his house, burned the house and people in it, and killed his wife and son and a number of his followers. Gissur himself escaped death by hiding in a vat of sour whey sunk in the floor and covered with a lid. He gathered forces again and began to hunt down and kill his attackers. Gissur went again to Norway, where Hákon gave him the title of jarl and assigned him the southern quarter, the northern quarter, and the western section of Iceland. After four years, he returned home to Iceland. Isolating and killing those who opposed him, he consolidated his holdings and power. For the first time in about four hundred years, Iceland was united under the rule of a single earl, appointed by and ruling on behalf of the king of Norway. The year was 1264.

Thus ended a period of bloody double-crosses, burnings, and murders, a time of chaos that took its name, Sturlunga period, from Snorri's relatives, the descendants of Sturla, who were the most powerful family in Iceland for most of the thirteenth century. They were also one of the most literary families in Icelandic history. Sturla, the son of Þórður by his mistress, lived between 1214 and 1284. Þórður was the son of Sturla and brother of Snorri. The reason we know so much about the details of the Sturlung period (even the names of men who fought on each side of each battle, the number of combatants, the names of people's fathers, mothers, wives, husbands, and paramours) is that Sturla the grandson wrote the *Saga of the Icelanders*, a history of the period. Early in the fourteenth century this was assembled with a series of smaller sagas about individual chieftains and areas into a collection called the *Sturlunga Saga*, the saga of the Sturlungs.

I became interested in the Icelandic sagas indirectly. After doing intensive ethnographic fieldwork among the tribal Lisu of northern Thailand I was reading other anthropologists' works to expand my understanding of what I had experienced when I read Rosalie Wax's book *Magic, Fate, and History* about medieval Iceland and its worldview and Victor Turner's essay "An Anthropological Approach to the Icelandic Saga." Turner (1971: 351) says that he shifted his interest from literature to anthropology in part to work in a society "not too dissimilar to ancient Iceland." From his detailed ethnographic fieldwork among Ndembu, Turner found the sagas familiar and concluded that they were good models of and for medieval Icelandic social life.

I read *Njáll's Saga* and found in it many of the same kinds of events and ideas I had witnessed among Lisu. There were intricate legal cases like ones I had seen and recorded, eloquent testimony of witnesses and advocates, appeals to custom and law, factions that hated each other with a vengeance, and stories of feuds and killings. There were people like Njáll, wise in their customs, understanding people's motivations so well that they could predict their reactions, who advised and counseled others. Among Lisu there were no police or courts, no government to appeal to if people's negotiated settlements broke down. Lisu were not organized as a state. To appeal to Thai lowlanders was for everyone to lose, a price no one was willing to pay.

I saw a sorcerer make curses to harm another person, and others, deathly afraid of the consequences, appeal to him not to take human life, though he could. There were defenses against sorcery.

Daily, spirits would possess and ride shamans as their horses. The ghost of a recently dead man haunted the village, especially a place just behind my house, on the way from his house to his fields. I heard stories of people who had banded together to hunt down and kill others who had wronged them. Once a traveler came to my house. After the custom, I offered him refreshment and asked the news and his business. He inquired after a person for whom he was looking and explained he was going to kill him in vengeance.

I saw lowland traders, like the Norwegian traders who came to Iceland, systematically misunderstand Lisu. I saw how important seating arrangements at feasts and festivals were and attended wedding feasts as well as divorce cases. I observed and recorded cases of manslaughter, killings, and compensations, dowry negotiations. There were cases in which well-known advocates remained neutral because of conflicting kinship connections, cases whose intricacies rested on complex genealogical relationships and historical relationships among groups. In the sagas I saw such events and patterns recorded not by an alien anthropologist, but by the people who had experienced them.

Not only that—I had read accounts by many other anthropologists who had recorded similar things of similar peoples around the world. Because I had lived in a society in which witches, sorcerers, ghosts, feuds, hauntings, factions, and vengeance were daily realities, the sagas seemed true and believable to me. There were several big differences. Among Lisu there were no chieftains or aristocrats, no concepts of hierarchy, and no concept of land as property one could own.

Later I did ethnographic work among lowland Shan in northwestern Thailand, people who do have well-developed concepts of hierarchy, property, and courts and government institutions to enforce them. This was the big difference between Shan and the people of the Icelandic sagas, who had no state institutions. Shan elders, men and women, told stories of times past they could remember of Shan princes and their conflicts, their levies of forced labor and taxes, and their festive travels through their principalities like the Norwegian kings of the Icelandic sagas. Such feasts are recorded in *Egill's Saga* when the king of Norway, a figure much like a Shan prince, traveled through his realm. Suspicious that Þórólfur, Skalla-Grímur's brother, resented his visits and his rule, the king killed him. Feasts can be less festive than burdensome to those who must furnish the provisions.

Subsequently I went to Iceland to study fishing, studied Icelandic, and worked on a couple of farms to learn about the language, outlook, and farm practices of modern Icelanders. Then my interest in medieval Icelandic literature was rekindled.

During the Sturlung period warfare escalated. Chieftains kept more and more followers. Their households became armed camps. In the fragile subarctic ecosystem of Iceland, providing food for such nonproductive persons became a problem and often enough they simply pillaged from the nearest farmers.

Norwegian traders found the trip to Iceland increasingly profitless. There was no market economy there. The exchange values of goods against one another and standard exchange values were negotiated at assemblies. This was not always to the liking or benefit of traders. They came to Iceland less and less frequently with needed cargos of grain to supplement the diet, timber for building, and luxury goods for chieftains to display and give away in social exchange.

Thus, both internal dynamics and the place of Iceland in Europe's changing international economy propelled Iceland toward incorporation with Norway. Later, Norway was incorporated into Denmark, and Icelanders began to look upon Gissur Þorvaldsson not as the one who ended internal strife and external trading difficulties, but as the one who delivered them into the hands of the harsh colonial master.

While the Sturlung age was a period of internecine warfare, strife, cruelty, shortsighted selfishness, and violence, it was also an age of great writing. In the Sturlung period, Icelanders turned their attention to their past and wrote sagas about their own ancestors, the Norse settlers who came to Iceland in the ninth century from Norway and the British Isles.

The traditionally accepted date for the first permanent settlement is 874. Settlers claimed land on the uninhabited island and established an agricultural economy based largely on grass. They raised sheep, cattle, horses, and in places some grain as well. The land was all claimed by 930 when the general assembly (Alþing) was founded, thus marking the end of the period of settlement. In the year 1000, by a compromise decision of a single arbiter selected at the Alþing, Christianity became the religion of Iceland. Individual farmers built and maintained Christian churches.

The tithe law of 1096 provided that tax-paying farmers would contribute 1 percent of the assessed value of their property each year to be divided into four parts: one for the church, one for the bishops, one for the clergy, and one for the poor. The church owners, most of whom were chieftains and influential in the Alþing, received the shares for the churches and clergy and benefited as much as anyone from the tax. Furthermore, lands that belonged to a church were not taxable, so some landowners donated their land to the church, maintained control of it as managers, and benefited doubly. This process aided the concentration of land into a few hands. There is plenty of evidence that things did not run as smoothly as the laws would indicate, that collecting the taxes was a sometime thing, and that church owners did not always support the bishops or the poor.

In the early period, when land was plentiful, labor limits put ceilings on production. One could not recruit labor outside the household. As long as there was land to be claimed, no one would work for someone else while it was possible to work for oneself and keep the product for one's own use. While slaves augmented the size of households so that one could claim and work larger tracts of land with them than without them, they also proved a liability because they ate about as much as they produced. By the year 1000 some families were working land that was insufficient to meet their consumption needs. It was not possible to intensify production. The major product was livestock, which depended on grass. The amount of grass, especially grass that one could save as hay to bring livestock through the winters, put an absolute limit on the number of stock a household could maintain. Households with less than enough land could send some of their members to work at larger establishments in exchange for their keep during part of the year.

The tithe law of 1096 provided that one-fourth of the revenues collected were to be used to support the poor of the communities from which they were collected. This indicates that there were people who found it difficult to support themselves through the year and that the landowners, those chieftains and worthy men who made the laws, found it to their benefit to maintain them by taxing others so that they would be available for labor when needed. This made less demand on their household funds than the support of slaves, without affecting productivity. The difference could be used for alternate purposes. For large and powerful households such alternative uses included sponsoring periodic feasts, presenting lavish gifts to others of the same class to cement alliances, and paying large fines to avoid fights when they chose to. This "addition" to the funds of independent households provided an exploitable resource for chieftains and large landowners. After the year 1000 slaves were freed and replaced with seasonal labor.

With seasonal labor available, large landowners could expand their holdings and thus increase their power not only by controlling land but through gifts, dowry and bride prices for marriages, and other distributions. They did this by gaining control of land from those who had insufficient land to support their households. While there had originally been slaves and freepeople, owners of larger or smaller estates, now various other nonlandowning categories developed.

This system, in both its economic and political aspects, relied on the concept of property. Rents and recompense for labor, as well as differential access to land, depended on the property relationships. Though the concept was defined in law, the law was ultimately unenforceable. There was no institutional form to enforce it, only the system of private vengeance, which could receive public sanction through legal maneuverings at the various assemblies. There was no state to give institutional reality to the concept of property.

This social and economic process provided the material from the pre-Sturlung times for the sagas known as family sagas. The most famous of these are *Njáll's Saga, Egill's Saga, Gísli's Saga, Eyrbyggja Saga*, and *Laxdæla Saga*. The first three are named for their major characters, while the second two are named for areas.

*Njáll's Saga* is the longest and most intricately wrought of the family sagas. One of its central characters, Gunnar, is the archetype of the saga hero. He is handsome, accomplished, well traveled, very athletic, somewhat modest, and not very clever. After he returns from successful travels abroad, he goes to a meeting of the general assembly dressed in his newly acquired finery. He is the talk of the assembly and the best-dressed person there. He meets an equally well-dressed woman, tall, blonde, and beautiful, named Hallgerður. Hallgerður, the daughter of Höskuldur and niece of his half-brother and friend Hrútur, has had a series of unfortunate marriages: her husbands have been killed by her oversensitive foster father for what he takes to be insults to her.

Gunnar's advisor in all matters is the wise and prescient Njáll, who advises against the marriage. Gunnar does not listen, and Hallgerður gets him involved in disputes with others, including Njáll himself. He is able to keep his relationship with Njáll on good terms because Njáll knows about his problems, but he gets involved in feuds with others, which end in his being outlawed. At one point he slaps Hallgerður, an act that has caused the death of a former husband. Outlawed, he refuses to leave his farm at Hlíðarendi. Since he does not leave, anyone can kill him with impunity. His many friends offer him help, which he refuses. His enemies attack him in his house. He holds them off with his bow and arrows until an attacker leaps up and cuts his bowstring. Then he asks his wife to cut a length of her long hair and plat it into a bowstring for him. She reminds him of the time he slapped her and refuses to help. He defends himself valiantly, but his enemies kill him in the end.

Then the saga shifts to Njáll and his sons, who fall under the influence of a scheming and jealous chieftain, Mörður. Their foster brother is a chieftain who is growing daily in popularity while the scheming chieftain is losing followers. Mörður convinces the brothers that their foster brother is plotting against them, and they kill him. This leads to a series of events that culminate when the enemies of Njáll burn him and his family in their house. One son-in-law escapes. The remainder of the saga details his vengeance, how he hunts down the burners and kills them. Finally he is reconciled with the leader of the burners and marries his niece, the widow of the murdered foster brother.

If Gunnar is the model of the fair-haired hero, Egill is the antithesis. He is ungenerous, covetous, moody, irritable, temperamental, proud, often despondent, clever, and a great poet.

Egill was the son of Skalla-Grímur (Grim the bald), whose father was Kveld-úlfur (evening wolf, because he was something of a werewolf). Never a follower of King Haraldur, Kveld-úlfur fell out with him when the king killed his favorite son, Þórólfur. After taking vengeance on the king's followers, Kveld-úlfur dies on the way to Iceland and Skalla-Grímur establishes a new farm there.

The saga is especially detailed in its description of the economic basis of the new farm. Egill, like his father and grandfather, is gloomy, somber, and swarthy while his brother, like his father's brother, is blond, outgoing, and handsome. Egill goes to Norway with his brother, but gets involved in many adventures which alienate him from the king.

Unwelcome in Norway, the brothers pillage and raid and then go to England to fight on the side of King Aðalsteinn against the Scots. When his brother is killed in battle, Egill goes to Norway to take care of his brother's estate and marry his widow. After his wife's father dies, one of her sisters' husbands takes his whole estate. Egill returns to claim his wife's share, but ends up killing King Eiríkur's son and several of his followers.

When his father dies, Egill takes over his estate and goes abroad again, only to fall into the hands of the hated King Eiríkur, who is now in England. He saves his life by the intervention of a friend and by making a poem of lavish sycophantic praise for the king. Egill is involved in more inheritance claims in Norway, raids some more, and returns to Iceland to grow old.

He is inconsolable when one of his sons drowns, but his daughter, Þorgerður, cajoles him back from his depression and he makes a poem for his son, in which he laments that he cannot take revenge on the sea. Another son is the father of Helga the fair, who is the central woman in *Gunnlaugur's Saga*. Old, blind, and helpless, Egill dies at home.

Gísli, the central figure of the saga of that name, is not as brooding as Egill, but he is far from the model hero. He runs from his pursuers when he has a chance to escape. He sometimes uses other people badly, sacrificing them for his own benefit. And yet, perhaps because he is an underdog, we feel sympathy for him.

*Gísli's Saga* also starts in Norway, where a disappointed suitor of his sister tries to burn his family in their house. They escape, burn the burners, and then go to Iceland. After the parents die, the three siblings get married. The brothers work the same farm, just next to that of their sister's husband, Þorgrímur. Gísli travels abroad with his wife's brother, Vésteinn, while Gísli's brother, Þorkell, travels with Þorgrímur.

After they return, Þorkell overhears his wife telling Gísli's wife that she loves Vésteinn, Gísli's wife's brother. Þorkell divides the family wealth and moves in with Þorgrímur next door. Vésteinn comes to Gísli's place for a feast, but someone sneaks into the house and stabs him to death in his bed. Gísli knows the killer is Þorgrímur, because Þorkell is related by marriage to Vésteinn and cannot kill him but Þorgrímur is not, so Þorkell has persuaded Þorgrímur to kill his rival. Gísli waits until there is another feast at his brother's farm, then sneaks into the house at night and kills Þorgrímur with the same spear he used on Vésteinn.

Gísli's sister marries Þorgrímur's brother, Börkur. A sorcerer casts a spell on the killer of Þorgrímur, that he will receive no aid. Gísli's sister realizes that Gísli killed her husband when he makes a careless verse about it. When she tells her husband, he gets Gísli outlawed and begins to hunt him down.

Gísli evades his hunters for years by clever tricks. Finally Gísli and his wife settle in an out-of-the-way valley in the West Fjords, but Börkur's followers find Gísli and attack him. He makes a valiant defense, aided by his always loyal wife, but his attackers kill him. The saga writer observes that Gísli, on the run for eighteen years and finally hunted down and killed by his pursuers, was not in all things a lucky man.

When the man who killed Gísli reports his success to Börkur, Gísli's sister Þórdís tries to kill him and divorces Börkur. She is the mother of Snorri the chieftain, who is a central figure in *Eyrbyggja Saga*. Snorri is quite unlike Gunnar, Egill, and Gísli. He is neither moody nor brooding, but bright, alert, always scheming. He has Njáll's understanding of social relations and, like Njáll, advises others to their advantage, but he is no fighter like Gunnar, Egill, and Gísli.

The saga explains how the Snæfellsnes peninsula was settled by Norse chieftains fleeing King Haraldur of Norway and relates their feuds in Iceland. Among the settlers is Þórólfur, whose grandson was the Þorgrímur who married Gísli's sister, whose son was Snorri the chieftain. After a trip to Norway, Snorri manages to trick his dead father's brother, now his mother's husband, Börkur, out of his farm at Helgafell. There are witches, sorcerers, unmanageable berserkers from Norway, feuds, seductions, piratical raids on farmers, assassination attempts, killings, fights with very concrete ghosts (not ethereal beings), hauntings, and Eiríkur the red from the West Fjords is outlawed and sails to Greenland. Through all of this Snorri the chieftain advises, helps, makes alliances, and takes cases to the assembly.

Snorri the chieftain has a similar role in *Laxdæla Saga*, whose central character is Guðrún, the daughter of Ósvífur. The saga opens with Norse chieftains leaving because of Haraldur. They go to the British Isles, but after some years move to Iceland. The main person to go to Iceland was Unnur the deep-minded, a very dignified and powerful woman who dies at the wedding feast of her grandson. Her granddaughter Þorgerður marries and has a son named Höskuldur, familiar from *Njáll's Saga*. After her husband dies, her son takes over Unnur's establishment. Hallgerður, Gunnar's wife in *Njáll's Saga*, is his daughter.

Þorgerður goes to Norway, remarries, and has another son, Hrútur, also familiar from *Njáll's Saga*. In this saga the two brothers quarrel over their inheritance after Hrútur goes to Iceland. Höskuldur buys a slave girl on a trading trip and brings her back to Iceland, where his wife receives her coldly. The slave, who turns out to be not the common slave she appears to be, but the daughter of the king of Ireland, has a son named Óláfur.

Óláfur goes to visit his grandfather, the Irish king, who acknowledges him, and returns to Iceland to marry Þorgerður, Egill's daughter from *Egill's Saga*, the one who roused him from his depression after his son drowned. Óláfur becomes one of the most famous of the Icelandic chieftains, mentioned in many sagas.

They have a son named Kjartan. Meanwhile, Höskuldur's son by his wife, Þorleikur, has a son named Bolli. Þorleikur is angry when Höskuldur includes his illegitimate son Óláfur in his will, so Óláfur offers to foster Bolli to make their relationship closer. Bolli and Kjartan grow up as brothers.

They both fall in love with Guðrún, daughter of Ósvífur. When they go to Norway, Kjartan tries to get Guðrún to promise to wait for him for three years, but she will not, though she loves him. In Norway, Kjartan takes up with the sister of the king. Bolli returns first and tells Guðrún that he thinks Kjartan will stay with the king's sister. Guðrún marries Bolli because she thinks Kjartan no longer cares for her. When Kjartan returns, she goads Bolli and her brothers into killing Kjartan, who does not even fight back against his beloved foster brother, but dies at his hand.

Þorgerður, Egill's daughter, the dead Kjartan's mother, goads her other sons into killing Bolli in revenge. They find Bolli and Guðrún in their summer livestock tending house, a shieling. Guðrún carefully notes the killers. One of them wipes Bolli's blood from his sword on Guðrún's sash and predicts that the avenger is even now under the sash.

Guðrún names her son Bolli after his father and trades farms with Snorri the chieftain, who acts as her advisor to concoct a plan to get a suitor to help her young son avenge his father. After they take vengeance, the suitor is killed. Guðrún marries again, and her husband drowns. Her son marries Snorri's daughter and goes on a pilgrimage. Guðrún becomes a nun, but before she dies her son asks which of her men she loved the most. She replied that she loved most the one she treated worst.

There are about thirty family sagas in all. The same people appear in different sagas. Snorri the chieftain shows up in *Njáll's Saga* and others; Hallgerður plays a major role in *Njáll's Saga* but is only mentioned in *Laxdæla Saga*; the half brothers Hrútur and Höskuldur who are at odds in *Laxdæla Saga* are portrayed as very close in *Njáll's Saga*.

*Hen-Þórir's Saga* (*Hænsa-Þórir's Saga*) indicates tension between the chiefly model of political economy and attempts by some from the lower orders to establish an alternative in the crevices. High value is placed on entourage building by arranging marriages and

foster relationships, but there is nothing but scorn for the merchant Þórir, who is despised because he follows a commercial
rather than a social logic.

*Bandamanna Saga* is a satire which derives its humor from its
treatment of reciprocity and other dimensions of honor. It offers
an opposition to the Gunnar-like image of saga-age heroes and
satirizes the political leaders of the thirteenth century as greedy,
selfish, and honorless.

Other sagas tell of the ill-fated love lives of the poets Kormákur
and Gunnlaugur. Still others relate Eiríkur the red's discovery and
colonization of Greenland and his son Leifur's and others' expeditions to Vínland.

While the sagas are presented in a very objective-sounding
style, describing only actions and discourse, never thoughts or
feelings, and never taking the omniscient view of a novelist who
knows all of the relationships and how things will turn out, it is
quite clear who they favor and who they do not. There is no
doubt that Hallgerður is a wicked woman. There is no question
that Guðrún is a heroine. Both women are much alike in their
comportment, but they are judged radically differently. The saga
writers let their audience know their judgments of people by putting words in the mouths of "the people of the countryside,"
by having a character comment "you are a wicked woman" as
Gunnar's mother tells Hallgerður, and by their descriptions of
characters as popular versus unpopular, fair versus overbearing,
thoughtful versus unthoughtful, sociable versus unsociable, generous versus stingy, and so on.

Sagas are not novels. They are not even like novels. They have
no suspense, no character development, no plot lines. A saga is
frustrating at first reading because the writer assumes the reader
is already familiar with it. The genealogies are confusing and seem
irrelevant at first until one is halfway through and realizes that a
familiar pattern is showing up again. Sagas cannot be read quickly
like novels. They must be savored and read again and again until
they become like old friends, until one knows not only what is
happening now but what is going to happen and what has happened in the past, and who is related to whom in what ways.
Then, accepted on their own terms, they begin to make sense not

so much as stories about characters, as I have presented them in synoptic form here, but as intricately wrought structures.

One begins to see that Egill repeated the major aspects of his father's ambivalent relations with the kings of Norway, that his father repeated his father. The pattern perpetuates itself. Njáll could see into the future and knew what would happen. He tried his best to save his friend Gunnar, but he could not. He tried to save his own family, but could not. The same thing that happened to Gísli's family in Norway repeated itself in Iceland. The same sword his father's brother broke in a dispute with its owner, reforged into a short spear by a sorcerer, killed Vésteinn and Þorgrímur. Sagas do not tell stories, they describe patterns. There is no suspense in a pattern—there is repetition until one sees and understands it.

Sagas are not for everyone, especially given the tastes of today's fast-paced world. But for those who can take the time and have the patience to savor them, to read them again and again until the patterns become apparent, they reveal life in a society quite different from ours, with an economy based on social relations rather than on markets; a politics based on fosterage and marriage as well as feast sponsoring and gift giving; a social order based on reciprocity; a law with intricate customary procedures (if you won you had to enforce your own court victory since there were no police to call and no jails for outlaws)—a society that appreciated enduring patterns and thought itself part of such patterns laid down in the custom and practice of the past.

Were Höskuldur and Hrútur really friends as in *Njáll's Saga* or enemies as in *Laxdæla Saga*? How can we believe both? We do not need to believe both. We need only understand what it meant to be a friend and what it meant to be an enemy. The sagas may not be "true" by modern standards of historical reportage. The only way to judge is to compare their contents with the equally contestable contents of other documents such as law books and chronicles, which often enough confirm events and individuals, but not always. The *Sturlunga Saga* gives us contemporary or near contemporary accounts of events, but they are not therefore more or less reliable. They are the accounts of a people told to themselves and by themselves. Furthermore, they were a people radically different in their assumptions and outlook from modern people.

If we read the family sagas and *Sturlunga Saga* for their patterns, to understand the political and economic systems that produced them and the assumptions upon which they are based in terms of what we know from anthropology about other such societies, we can build a picture of the society of the time and how it evolved from the first chieftains who settled on the island to the chaos of the Sturlung times and its incorporation into Norway.

If we accept this literature for what it is, it opens a window on a vastly different world from our modern one. The sagas show us men and women in action, patterns in existence, and many examples of grace under pressure. While they are remote from our world, they are not irrelevant.

Many sagas are available in translations. I first became sensitized to issues of translation when the Icelandic literary historian Ástáður Eysteinsson and I taught a course on Icelandic sagas together. We spent hours discussing each saga from various points of view, literary, historical, and anthropological. Our class texts were English translations of the sagas. Frequently Ástáður would indignantly proclaim that the whole sense of the English text was very misleading because of mistranslation. He explained numerous examples in detail.

From an anthropological perspective, I had identified systematic projections of state- or market-related concepts onto a nonstate and nonmarket system. For instance, to translate "wealth" as "money" is to suggest a modern market concept in place of the more relevant notions of livestock or woolen goods. To translate "landowning farmer's son" as "peasant's son" is a drastic change of social status. Even to translate "landowning farmer" as "farmer" misses the significant social, political, and economic dimension of the relevant status and fails to communicate the position and importance of landownership.

I became even more sensitive to translation issues when Dorothy Durrenberger and I analyzed the translations of *Gunnlaugur's Saga*, which we selected because it is the saga that has been most translated into English so we could compare several different translation policies. How people translate reflects how they understand the material they are translating. Translations are not neutral. We found that none of the translations was adequate (Durrenberger and Durrenberger 1986).

Eiríkr Magnússon and William Morris (1891) and Guðbrandur Vigfússon and F. York Powell (1905) used free translation and archaisms to evoke a spirit of an earlier time. More recent translators such as Magnus Magnusson and Herman Pálsson (1969), Herman Pálsson and Paul Edwards (1973), Gwyn Jones (1935), and Alan Boucher (1983) use free translation to attempt to move the sagas toward being modern novels. A much criticized alternative has been translation which is neither self-consciously modern nor archaic, such as George Johnston's (1963) translation of *Gísli's Saga*. All agree that the translations in the archaic style are very inaccessible (Calder 1970; Maxwell 1961; Swannell 1961). Readers have to try to comprehend an unfamiliar language which is neither Icelandic nor English. While the modernizations make texts accessible, they obscure and distort the originals (Johnston 1961; Durrenberger and Durrenberger 1986).

Close translations are an alternative. While they must differ from modern literary models to reflect the sagas, they need be neither unreadable nor grotesque. This approach can provide an accessible text and allow the original to show through (Johnston 1961). Some translators, concluding that the Icelandic sagas are not "literary" enough, have endeavored to "improve" them in translation to hold up the reputation of medieval Icelandic literature as a great or world literature. In doing so, they have neglected the social and cultural context of the sagas.

Commonwealth Iceland had no state. That fact puts the society, ideology, culture, and cultural artifacts squarely in the realm of what some have called the "primitive." While this designation may be offensive to some, it is not to anyone who has viewed close up the genius such people have for law, negotiation, poetry, song, and other cultural forms which we of modern societies value.

Traditional schools of literary criticism, literary scholarship, and folklore, like saga scholarship, have insisted that "the text is the thing" (Limón and Young 1986). More modern approaches emphasize understanding "artistic act, expressive form, and esthetic response, . . . in terms of locally defined, culture-specific categories and contexts" (Paredes and Bauman 1972: xi). This view is congenial to anthropologists who describe and analyze locally defined culture-specific categories and contexts (Geertz 1973), who are used to "strange perceptions and stranger stories" (Geertz 1983: 4). Clifford Geertz (1983: 119) argues that in the absence of such contextual knowledge of the culture and society the foreigner's response to its arts can only be "ethnocentric sentimentalism." He points out the double narrowing that results from the severance of the study of meaning fixed in inscriptions from the study of the social processes that fix it (1983: 32).

One of the problems of translation is that Old Icelandic is not a living language. Icelandic social, political, and economic forms of recent centuries have been quite different from those characteristic of the time when the sagas were written or about which they were written. While the best guide to the grammar of the language is living Icelandic, the best guide for translating and understanding this literature is the comparative study of social, political, and economic systems similar to the medieval Icelandic ones, such as those modern anthropologists study.

In modern anthropology, translation is a central issue (Sahlins 1972: 149–184; Becker 1984), but the comparative study of social and cultural systems to understand "locally defined, culture-specific categories and contexts" (Parades and Bauman 1972: xi) is foreign to the saga scholarship that has informed translations, if not all saga scholarship, and the text remains "the thing," isolated from social and cultural context and "improved" to make it fit some imagined standards of greatness, which the translators find wanting in the original texts. Ignorant of cultural, political, religious, economic, aesthetic, and folkloric contexts apart from their own modern ones, translators have been largely incapable of preserving the cultural form of the sagas. The sagas are beyond their range of actual and vicarious experience.

If I had worked in terms of the assumptions of the modernizing translators to describe the religion of the tribal Lisu of the highlands of northern Thailand, I would have described their shamans as Christian clergy because that is what my American and European readers are familiar with, what they would expect on the basis of their experience. Had I used the assumptions of the earlier translators, I would have used the imagery of Old Testament prophets. I would have omitted encounters with sorcerers, hauntings, spirits riding shamans, and other events which Lisu found reasonable and natural because they might seem bizarre, improbable, or grotesque to European and American readers. Neither approach would be accurate. Both would distort the cultural reality I attempted to describe and explain. Rather, I developed a description of Lisu society and culture, of Lisu life, so that a description of Lisu shamans and other categories in Lisu terms would be intelligible to my contemporaries. This is the approach I would like to see in saga translation.

Some argue that one must sacrifice either a readable English text or a close approximation to the original. Others (like Johnston 1961) call for a translation policy that circumvents the difficulties with archaisms but avoids the inaccuracies of the more modern translations.

Free translations, archaic or modern, distort the worldview of the sagamen as well as their literary works. The way a saga is told and the details of its structure and texture transmit cultural information which translations have distorted. Durrenberger and Durrenberger's detailed study of translation issues (1986) indicates that the sagas convey cultural information by their shifting tenses, formulaic openings, details of word choice, and lack of subordinate clauses, all features which are distorted or obliterated in translations, but which indicate the "totemic" nature of the sagas and communicate details of social, economic, political, and religious life.

In anthropology, textual translation is usually used in the service of cultural description, a broader translation project. An anthropologist describes aspects of a cultural system and uses translations of documents, sayings, discourses, and other texts as illustrations or sources of information about cultural patterns. Translations are thus embedded in a cultural analysis as illustration, example, or data. The sagas have not been translated in this tradition. Rather, the context of their translation has been literary or historical. Most translators have been concerned to transform the sagas from what they are into the translator's vision of what they ought to be, an image of a form of literature that can be considered great by modern standards.

Vigfússon and Powell (1905) suggest that *Hávarður's Saga* must be a degenerated sixteenth-century collage of mistakes, copies of parts of other sagas, and inventions of copyists to fill in blanks in the manuscripts from which they copied. The translators straightforwardly assert their concept of what a saga should "naturally" be and, to the extent that the manuscripts depart from their model, judge the text to be faulty. The realities of the text must bend before the preconceptions of its translators. They consider some events to be "preposterous," and everything beyond chapter 10 to be absurd or "monstrously improbable." Vigfússon and Powell take it upon themselves to eliminate all the fights with ghosts and other absurdities from the saga. In their translation, they eliminate the "contributions" they imagine their inventive scribe made to the final degenerate saga they had in front of them. While scribes were imaginative and creative enough to fill in gaps and to contribute interpretations here and there, some others must have been considerably less creative, because they produced "a number" of identical paper copies. Rather than taking this as evidence that the saga had some kind of coherence for its audience, enough to be recognized and copied for some reason, Vigfússon and Powell follow the tradition of their imaginary creative scribe and change the text to fit their preconceived notions of what a "proper" saga should be. Modern translators continue in the same tradition. Magnusson and Pálsson (1969: 43) find genealogies irrelevant to the stories and relegate them to footnotes to avoid irritating the sensibilities of modern readers. This is extreme distortion.

Magnússon and Morris had more respect for the text and at least translate all of it, though their translations are at times fanciful. One cannot demand a word-for-word translation because it sometimes takes more than one English word to translate an Icelandic word and several Icelandic words may translate as a single English one. But both of these translators transformed the text more than the requirements of translation demanded. Except for Johnston, modern translators have done no better at preserving the cultural dimensions of the texts they have translated.

Important cultural information is lost by free translation. The consequence is that the free translation is much more than a translation—it is a transformation of the saga into another kind of cultural artifact, of the nineteenth or twentieth century rather than the twelfth or thirteenth. Those who appreciate the sagas as cultural documents rather than as decontextualized literature have an aesthetic sense that demands the closest translation possible given the limitations of the English language to fit into the Icelandic mold. If one's objective is to appreciate and understand cultural differences, then, the differences must be preserved, perhaps even accentuated, rather than obliterated.

In his discussion of translation of Tiv law concepts, Paul Bohannan reports that when someone claimed that Kant could be translated into Eskimo, Margaret Mead laconically replied, "Of course, but can you make an Eskimo understand it?" (Bohannan 1969: 411). Mead was not claiming that Eskimo lack the intellectual capacity to comprehend Kant. She was not denying that their language can encode the concepts of Kant. She was inquiring whether Eskimo would immediately have the appropriate cultural categories in terms of which Kant could possibly make sense. We have the same problem with Icelandic sagas. They can be translated into English. The problem is whether we can provide sufficient background and context to make them understandable to any modern audience steeped in the assumptions and presuppositions of state societies.

The major evidence for the period and its dynamics are linguistic—documents, texts. One of the fundamental problems is how to assess the relation between the family sagas and medieval Icelandic society. This question is a microcosm of the discussions about the relations among literature, history, and culture which have been going on in the literary, historical, and anthropological disciplines, each to some extent taking from the others (Hunt 1989).

Anthropologists are concerned with the same issues of the status of history. In the past, cultural anthropologists were likely to confine their analyses to a single period, usually based on a fairly short span of a year or two of fieldwork. Some such ethnographic accounts were what Raymond Williams (1977) calls epochal rather than dynamic. Archaeologists have always had a more dynamic view of social orders because they deal with longer time spans. In the United States, where archaeology is considered a part of anthropology, this has contributed to an awareness of historical process in other areas of the discipline.

More recently, cultural anthropologists are witnessing great changes among the people they study (Kottak 1983) as researchers have revisited the places of their fieldwork over longer periods. Cultural and social anthropologists have therefore been addressing questions of social dynamics and cultural change as these have become observable in the process of fieldwork. Other motives for understanding historical processes stem from world systems theory and various approaches to anthropological questions and materials that are explicitly historical (Wolf 1982).

Marshall Sahlins wants to understand how people interpret events according to their conceptual structures which incorporate the political, social, and religious order and how culture is re-ordered in the process. He asks how cultures change in the process of trying to stay the same (Sahlins 1985; Biersack 1989; Roseberry 1989). History is ordered differently in societies with different schemes of meaning; cultural schemes are historically ordered as people revalue meanings in their acting out of them (Biersack 1989: 86).

William Roseberry (1989: 6) reads Geertz as rejecting the natural science quest for law in favor of interpretations of the meanings people give their actions. History and culture become similar if not the same thing. The historical is the culturally situated. Gabrielle Spiegel (1990: 74) objects to such an approach: "What gets lost in the concentration on meaning in place of experience is the sense of social agency, of men and women struggling with the contingencies and complexities of their lives in terms of the fates that history deals out to them and transforming the worlds they inherit and pass on to future generations."

Reviewing similar ground from the point of view of medieval literary studies, Lee Patterson (1987: 62) suggests that "to adopt an interpretive method that assumes that history is not merely known through but constituted by language is to act as if there are no acts other than speech acts." He argues that, while people act and communicate in terms of symbolic forms, actions have "a palpable force and an intentional purposiveness, however we may finally come to understand them, that stand against the irresolutions and undecidabilities valued by contemporary techniques of interpretation." Economic, political, social, and material reality exists even if literary historians must perforce operate within the closed world of textuality (Patterson 1987: 63).

But literary historians need not operate in the closed world of textuality. There are at least two ways out. One is via archaeology (Hodges 1989) and the other is via comparative ethnography (Clover 1988). While these approaches cannot provide detailed chronological "contexts" within which to situate literary works, they can describe their social and cultural environments. At the same time, the comparative perspective moves beyond the limitations of "local" interpretations implied in Geertz's and Sahlins's historical works to more inclusive accounts.

It is a convention among saga scholars to believe the contemporary *Sturlunga Saga* but not necessarily the family sagas because they are about events that took place some two or three hundred years before the sagas were written. Some believe *Grágás*, a compilation of laws, is a charter for medieval Icelandic thought and practice, while others argue on internal and textual evidence that it could not have been.

Some saga scholars argue that the anonymous sagamen who set down the sagas were authors who composed their works; others, that they transmitted and reshaped preexisting traditional material (Clover 1985: 279). These are modern echoes of the older debate about whether the sagas represent the record of an oral tradition or the composition of a novel-like literature for entertainment (Byock 1984: 194). Carol Clover's (1985) and Jesse Byock's (1984) reviews show that such questions have structured saga scholarship for some decades both inside Iceland and out. The debate is meaningless because the central questions can never be answered. No amount of "evidence" or cleverness can decide the issue of whether there were oral versions of sagas before they were written or even establish a precise chronology.

Contemporary contextual approaches render the central questions of Old Norse studies irrelevant. Which version of a story is best, prior, original, or most literary is not an appropriate question since a story consists of all its versions and variants. Nearly thirty years ago Claude Lévi-Strauss (1963 : 216–217) suggested that where the elements of a story come from and their status as "objective" history are irrelevant to the understanding of their relations with each other and what the story does for its auditors, readers, tellers, writers, and their culture and society (Geertz 1973: 118).

While many saga scholars have been content to remain within their closed circle of textuality, some who tend more toward social and legal history have moved beyond the traditional questions of saga scholarship toward a more social view (Byock 1982, 1988; Clover 1988; Miller 1990) but have paid slight heed to anthropology. Anthropologists have not ignored medieval Iceland. L. H. Morgan described medieval Icelandic kinship in 1871 and, as George Rich (1989) shows, others have followed. Marcel Mauss (1967) quotes *Hávamál* as a primitive text on reciprocity in the opening of his famous essay on *The Gift* in 1923. Karl Lewellyn and E. Adamson Hoebel (1941) refer to Icelandic evidence in their classic study of Cheyenne law. Rosalie Wax and Laura Thompson wrote on medieval Iceland in the late 1960s, and Victor Turner and Knut Odner followed in the early 1970s. Some work by A. Ya. Gurevich (1969, 1971) of the Soviet Union shows anthropological influence. If this work has not had an impact on medieval Icelandic studies, it is not because it was incompetent, irrelevant, inaccessible, or did not exist, but because Old Norse scholars did not attend to it. These scholars are notorious for their rejection of anything beyond their traditional closed realm of questions and sources, as their reviews of the work of Odner (1974) show. Peter Hallberg (1974) castigates M. I. Steblin-Kamenskij (1973; see also 1982) for daring to suggest that medieval Icelanders and sagamen were primitive people whose psychology was different from that of modern people.

A more thorough assessment of the sagas as historical sources must rely on a description of the society that produced them, its ideology, and the role of the sagas for that society. This is necessarily a circular process because I must build a description of the social order on the sagas and then use that description to assess their historical credibility. But the process is no more circular than the traditional practice of referring questions of historicity to other documents. All documents of the period—family sagas, contemporary sagas, the *Book of Settlements*, the law books—were written by the people of the time and for the people of the time and therefore are artifacts of the same culture. To move among the categories of documents does not remove the circularity.

The way to break out of the circularity is through comparative study, by contextualizing medieval Iceland not as so many documents among documents, not as so many books among books, but as a social and political order among others of the same kind. That is the contribution of an anthropological approach.

I do not attempt a review of all literature relevant to the Icelandic saga tradition. It is massive, and the reviews of Carol Clover and John Lindow (1985) and Jesse Byock (1984) need no repetition. I have reviewed the contribution of anthropologists to the study of medieval Iceland elsewhere (1989). My greatest intellectual debts are to Knut Odner, Victor Turner, and A. Ya. Gurevich, all of whom developed alternative perspectives on medieval Iceland.

# 2. PRODUCTION

I n the last third of the ninth century Haraldur Finehair began to consolidate a kingdom of the independent chieftaincies of Norway. His victory in a battle at Hafrsfjörður around 885 marks his success. Icelandic historical tradition has it that the settlers came to Iceland to escape the tyranny of Haraldur. A passage from chapter 4 of *Egill's Saga* illustrates this account:

When he had become owner of the counties which had just come into his power, King Haraldur was very attentive about landed men and powerful landholders and all of those from whom he suspected some uprising was expected. Then he had everyone do one thing or the other: become his servants or go away from the land, and the third choice was to undergo hardship or lose life, and some were maimed hand or foot. King Haraldur became owner in every county of all family land rights and all land, settled and unsettled, and equally the sea and the waters and all landowners should be his tenants, also those who worked in the forest and salt makers and all hunters both on sea and land. Then all of them were subject to him.

And because of this hardship many men fled away from the land and then much uninhabited land was settled widely both east in Jamtaland and Helsingjaland and in the British Isles, the Hebrides, the Dublin district, Ireland, Normandy in France, Caithness in Scotland, the Orkneys and Shetland, and the Faroe Islands. And in that time Iceland was discovered.

The various chieftains and landowners that Haraldur was trying to consolidate into a kingdom were operating household economies, if sometimes larger in scope than an immediate family. At least some land was owned under the old rule of alodial land rights, which inhered in the family collectively and were inalienable from it as a unit. Haraldur's policy was to claim ownership of all land and all resources in the kingdom for himself and grant others the privilege of using it for livelihood in return for specified services. For the chieftains this was an invitation to join a royal ruling class and to provide administrative, fiscal, and military functions in return for privileged access to resources and revenues.

Haraldur could claim no legal or historical precedence for his claim to ownership, but he did manage to piece together a coalition of allies sufficient to back his claim with force. The choice would have been attractive to his allies as long as they remained in royal favor, but to those many who procrastinated, ignored, or resisted Haraldur's innovations because of isolation, family loyalty, or other ideological reasons the new political realities meant an increase in the costs of operating the economic unit and taxes, with no balancing increases in productivity, as Haraldur did nothing to reorder the system of production.

The economic logic of household production, outlined by A. V. Chayanov (1966; see Durrenberger 1980, 1984a; Tannenbaum 1984a, 1984b), is that levels of production are determined by the balance of need and expenditure of labor. Each such economic unit has an undifferentiated fund for meeting the culturally defined ritual, social, and consumption needs of its consumers; reproducing productive effort by replacing tools and stock; expanding operations; gaining access to productive resources (rents and taxes); and insuring against failures. Chayanov represents the level of such needs in any domestic production unit as a descending curve of marginal utility. The less of the fund a unit has, the more it needs the rest, but the more it has obtained, the less it needs the balance.

Since the fund can only be gained by the efforts of household members, each unit of the household fund is won by labor. Chayanov argued that the drudgery of labor increases geometrically with the amount of labor expended: the more work one has done, the less inclined one is to do more.

The intersection of these two curves defines the level of production beyond which, by this logic, it is not worth the effort to produce more. Households cease productive efforts when this bal-

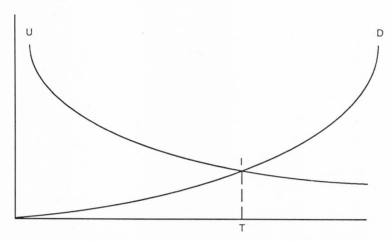

*Figure 1. How levels of production are determined in household production units. U = curve of marginal utility of goods, D = curve of marginal disutility of labor, I = intersection of U and D, T = production target.*

ance point has been reached (Durrenberger 1979, 1981, 1982a, 1984b; Durrenberger and Tannenbaum 1983, 1992). Figure 1 illustrates these relationships.

Anything that affects the productivity of labor affects the curve of the drudgery of labor. If some change allows the same amount of labor to produce twice as much value as before, the productivity of labor has doubled, and the drudgery halved. Anything which entails costs to the household, such as the price of more productive technology or the addition of consumers, increases the demands on the household fund and hence changes the position of its utility curve. The economic logic of households is to accept any change of its organization that allows for a better overall balance, that is, the same or more production at the same or lower levels of drudgery.

If a farm implement increases productivity to the point that the increased production required to pay for the implement (and the interest on the loan to get it in modern contexts) can be accomplished at a lower level of drudgery than the previous level of production without the implement, then the household will get the implement. Figure 2 illustrates such a situation.

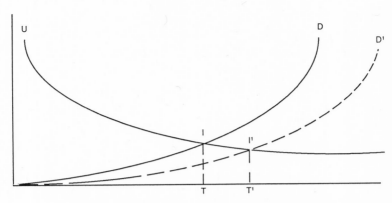

*Figure 2. Relative advantage is related to productivity in household production units. U = curve of marginal utility of goods, D = curve of marginal disutility of labor, D' = curve of marginal disutility of labor with greater productivity, I = intersection of U and D, I' = intersection of U and D', T = production target of I, T' = production target of I'.*

If, on the other hand, acquisition of the machine would establish a new balance at a higher level of drudgery, households would not acquire the implement.

Where there is choice, in situations of sparsely populated states or nonstate societies, social arrangements have the same impact as implements do in more modern contexts (Durrenberger 1984b). In at least some situations changes in political and social organization bring with them increases in productivity—for instance, the development of irrigation systems. Household units may well bear the costs of taxes and administration in return for more favorable production situations. In conditions of population sparsity, such as the early kingdoms of Southeast Asia, ruling classes must be careful that their appropriations from producers do not rise above the favorable balance point lest the population simply leave to colonize new areas.

In Norway, Haraldur offered nothing that would increase productivity. He offered some landowners the chance to share in increased appropriations from others as an inducement to join his coalition. To others, his innovations represented an increase in the level of utility curves with no offsetting increases in productivity, the establishment of a new balance of production at an unfavorable level. Hence, their choices were, as the Icelandic saga writer perceived: to join Haraldur, to leave the country, or to suffer hardship. Haraldur had claimed ownership of all of the resources of the area, the arable land, the forests, the fish, the salt. He backed his claim with victories against those who would dispute it.

There were other choices besides Iceland, as the sagaman indicates. But each of these choices offered additional costs that Iceland did not. In the other areas, one had the choice of joining an established political system and paying the required dues for access to resources or attempting to set oneself beyond or outside the system by force. This entailed the costs of either conquest or defense or both. In terms of the logic of household production, Iceland offered the best alternative, so many who tried to resettle in other areas came to Iceland within a few years.

Economic choices are usually conceived of and acted out in terms of political rhetoric, especially in systems such as this where there are no distinctions among the economic, political, and religious. If the logic of household economics was a significant reason for the migration to Iceland, we may expect that it continued to shape developments once the settlers arrived.

While chiefly households operated in terms of the logic of household economies, they incorporated subordinate households into their economic systems. Only chieftains had the wherewithal to consider such an option as relocating away from Haraldur. Subordinate households may have had a choice as to whether to go along or stay in Norway, but could not initiate such a move on their own. Chieftains did not go to Iceland alone but took subordinate households with them along with their slaves and householders so they could reestablish their economic systems in the new land. One could not be a chieftain without followers and dependent tributary households.

The units of production in medieval Iceland were households. According to the law book *Grágás*, independent households should have one cow-unit of productive capacity for each consumer-unit in the household. It further defined a boat or a net together with a debt-free draught animal and necessary farm implements as equivalent to a cow (Sveinsson 1953 : 49). The standard cow was between three and ten years old, able to bear calves and able to give milk enough for one calf in one day (Gelsinger 1981 : 36). The underlying idea of independence was the ability to produce sufficient food for the consumers of the household.

Chapter 29 of *Egill's Saga* describes how Skalla-Grímur established his farm:

> Skalla-Grímur was a very hard-working man. He always had many people with him, he had them seek many provisions. . . . But the livestock that there were then went all winter fending for themselves in the woods. . . . driftwood was not lacking west of Mýrar. He had a farm built on Alftanes and had another farm there, had people go fishing from there and hunt seals and the eggfields from there, as then [at that time] there was enough of all of these provisions. . . . There were also many drift whales and one could shoot as he wanted. Everything there in the hunting place was still because they were unused to people. . . . Skalla-Grímur also had his people up on salmon rivers to fish. He established Oddur lone-dweller on the Gjúfurá to take care of the salmon fishing there. . . .
>
> Then Skalla-Grímur had a farm built up by the mountains and had a farm there, had his sheep kept there. . . . Skalla-Grímur's means of wealth then stood on many feet.

Grass was the major crop, though there may have been some minor grain production. *Hávarður's Saga* indicates that people kept their livestock indoors during the winter and had sufficient labor to bring fodder to them. A household had to control enough pasture land to produce sufficient hay to feed the sheep and cattle until spring pasturage became available. Hay plays a major part in several sagas. In *Hávarður's Saga* as well as *Víga-Glúmur's Saga*, contested meadows are the cause of killing. Toward the end (chap. 84) of *Egill's Saga*, Egill's son, Þorsteinn, defends his pasture against the encroachments of his neighbor Steinar:

> "It is so," says Þorsteinn, "that I killed your slave last summer, the one you had graze the cattle on my land and then I let you graze as you wanted all the way to winter. Now I have killed another of your slaves for you. I gave to this the same fault as the other before. Now you shall

have grazing here the rest of the summer as you want, but next summer, if you graze my land and send people to herd your stock to this place, then I will again kill for you whomever of them who leads the stock, even if you lead yourself. I will do so every summer while you hold to your habit about the grazing."

In *Hen-Þórir's Saga* there is a poor crop of grass and little chance to dry it. Chieftain Blund-Ketill visits his tenants in the fall to collect his hay-rents from them and to determine how much livestock they would slaughter so that they could bring the remainder through the winter with the available hay. Some of his tenants ignore his advice and run out of hay in the winter.

The amount of pasture determined the amount of hay a household could produce, and the amount of hay determined the amount of livestock it could bring through the winter.

In the summer, people marked their sheep and took them to graze on marginal lands where the grass was too sparse and poor to be harvested. In the fall, as *Hávarður's Saga* tells, people rounded up all the sheep and separated them, each to its owner. After the roundup people killed the sheep they did not intend to carry through the winter. They had to match their sheep to the hay they had. The more hay, the larger a herd they could keep. The larger the herd of mature female sheep, the larger the number of spring lambs. People castrated the male lambs before taking them to the summer pasture. The more spring lambs, the more meat.

The hay had to be divided among horses, cattle, and sheep. The horses were important for display and transportation of people and goods as well as consumption. Chapter 2 of *Hen-Þórir's Saga* tells how chieftain Blund-Ketill had to kill the forty worst of his hundred and sixty horses to free hay for his tenants' livestock. Given a finite supply of hay, the more of any one kind of livestock a household kept, the less of the others it could keep.

The amount of hay a household could produce depended not only on the amount of land it controlled but also on the amount of labor it could recruit. Land without labor to harvest its hay was useless. Bruce Gelsinger (1981) points out that the laborers necessary to harvest the hay ate as many extra provisions through the year as the extra hay they could produce would provide. The productivity of labor was not so high that slaves could provide much more than their own requirements. As long as householders had to support laborers through the whole year, as they did slaves, they could not add to their total annual production and additional tracts of land were of no use to them, if the household had sufficient provisions for itself. Therefore, if the population of slaves increased, it was controlled either by freeing some of the excess slaves or by exposure of infants. As excess slaves were freed, they claimed land. The more slaves were freed, the more land was claimed (Gelsinger 1981).

Hávarður claims unsettled land for a new farm in his saga, which mentions that he was the only new settler in the area, suggesting an awareness that new lands were not plentiful. In this saga there is a graduation from slaves to servants to dependent kinsmen, sons, daughters, nephews, nieces, brothers, sisters, and others, who worked on the farms gathering provisions, fishing, making hay, and tending to sheep in winter, spring, fall, and summer.

Gelsinger (1981) suggests that by the year 1000 some households had access to insufficient land to meet their needs. Chapter 4 of *Hrafnkell's Saga* tells us:

Þorbjörn had little wealth but many dependents. His son was named Einar, the oldest. He was big and well accomplished.

It was one spring that Þorbjörn spoke with Einar that he would look for some lodging, "because I do not need more farm labor than this household here can support but you are good to lodge. You are well accomplished. This command to go is not because of lack of love because you are the most useful of my children to me. More because of my lack of means and my poverty. But my other children are becoming workers and you are better to lodge than they are."

I have translated the Icelandic *vista* as "to lodge." It means to provision, to board, or to lodge with someone else and was used in connection with servants. Here Þorbjörn is sending his son to look for some work in return for which he can get food and lodging.

In chapter 36 of *Njáll's Saga*, we see a labor transaction when

Bergþóra takes on Atli. It is not in terms of an exchange of a wage for work, but provisions, lodging, and subsistence in return for work. This transaction strongly indicates that, while there were people without access to resources, there was not a market for labor, simply people looking for some way to gain subsistence from one day to the next.

Bergþóra asks Atli where he is from and where he is going. He says he is *vistlaus*, homeless, without provisions, and says he is looking for Njáll and his sons to find out if they would receive him *taka við mér*. She asks him what work he is suited for, *Hvað er þér hentast að vinna?* He says he is a fieldhand or a farmer *akurgerðarmaður* (*akur* = field; *akurgerð* = agriculture, making fields; *akurgerðamaður*, a man who does agriculture), though he can do many other things. He asks if she can and will receive (*taka við*) him, which she does if he will do whatever work she requires, including killing a man. When Bergþóra agrees that his compensation will be that of a free man if he is killed, he accepts, and the feud between Hallgerður and Bergþóra continues. His part in it costs Atli his life, but he gets his wish that the compensation paid for him is that of a free man, not a slave.

Landowners could take in labor for specific tasks and not support the workers through the whole year. Landowners began to free slaves, who joined the ranks of those with less than sufficient land and provided the supply of people who needed to increment their household production by seasonal work.

Those who controlled more land than their households could work could rent some of it to others under a variety of arrangements under which the landowner appropriated some of the renter's production in return for allowing access to land, as the example from *Hen-Þórir's Saga* illustrates.

Seasonal labor and rental arrangements both offered means for landowners to appropriate value produced by those who had less than sufficient land to provide their own subsistence. The landowners could use these provisions to increase their own production as a way to recruit and support followers.

In *Hávarður's Saga*, Hávarður and his nephews avenge the killing of Hávarður's son by killing his killer, the chieftain Þorbjörn, and some of his relatives. The killers then take refuge with another chieftain, Steinþór. Before the winter is out, these followers of Steinþór's have eaten all of his provisions, and he must appeal to his sister's husband for help. As in other such systems, the chieftain's main obligation was generosity and support, which required plentiful goods.

The more provisions a person has, the more followers he can support, and the stronger are the alliances he can make with others. The more followers and chieftains a chieftain can call on, the more secure is his claim to land in this stateless system. Hávarður, like many others mentioned in his saga, has to move from his farm because he cannot defend himself against his own chieftain, Þorbjörn. When his son begins to attract what appears to be a following and some local power, Þorbjörn kills him.

Besides cattle and sheep, another important source of provisions is fishing. Hávarður's wife, Bjargey, rows to sea and fishes with one helper for three years while her husband is incapacitated. Chapter 52 of *Eyrbyggja Saga* mentions a storage room for dried fish, and the next chapter tells how Þóroddur went to get dried fish with five other men. In chapter 54 they all drown and the boat and fish wash ashore, but the bodies disappear. The drowned men haunt the farm at Fróðá, but some kind of creature is in the dried fish storeroom making noise. When the people take the fish out, they find that the fish at the bottom have been eaten. Chapter 14 of *Laxdæla Saga* tells of a fishing station at Breiðafjörður.

In Breiðafjörður lies the fishing place which is called Bjarneyjar. The islands are many together and were very wealthy. In that time many people sought catches there. There was also a great crowd there in all seasons. Wise people found it very important that people had goodwill together in fishing places. It was then said that people would become unlucky in catch if they had disagreements. Most people also gave it good heed.

It is said that one summer Ingjaldur, chieftain of Sauðeyjar's brother Hallur, came to Bjarneyjar and intended to get provisions. He took a place with that man who is named Þórólfur. He was a Breiðafjörður man and he was nearly only a wealthless freedman though also a quick man. Hallur is there a while and it seems he is much in front of other men.

The two fall out over the division of the catch, and Þórólfur goes away angry at Hallur's insults. He waits for Hallur to come ashore after fishing one day and chops off his head.

Chapter 11 of *Njáll's Saga* relates how Hallgerður, married unwillingly to Þorvaldur, is extravagant with his provisions so that they run out of dried fish before spring. Þorvaldur and eight of his men row out to some islands about twenty-five miles away to get more dried fish. Þorvaldur slaps his wife in the exchange, and her foster father avenges the slap by killing her husband while he is collecting provisions.

The economic point is that these landowners controlled fishing areas and the boats and labor with which to fish. The fishermen also dried the fish, then the landowners could go to their fishing areas to replenish their supply of fish whenever they needed.

The boats are described as being six- or eight-oared. The catch was proportional to the labor expended fishing—the more labor used for fishing, the more fish one could store.

Households had to produce their own provisions. There was no market economy, as *Hen-Þórir's Saga* indicates; though individuals might sell small amounts of goods, one could not hope to provision a household from food purchases. Woolen goods, livestock, and precious metals were means of exchange by which people computed the magnitude of transactions. The major transactions were social ones. When Icelanders went to Norway, they took woolen goods with them to give to their hosts. They received gifts of timber and grain in return. This is the logic of reciprocity and hospitality rather than of the market. Within Iceland, exchanges were in terms of marriages, compensations for killings and other faults, gifts, and hospitality.

Contemporary and family sagas relate that travelers were lost at sea, captured into slavery, disappeared in foreign lands, or lost their wares while traveling, but they do not record that anyone lost a fortune by trading. In societies in which the market is the mechanism for accumulating wealth, trading is a risky venture, and there are stories of both great gains and losses at trading.

The great losses of fortune recorded in the sagas are social losses incurred by inattention to maintaining a sufficiently strong following or other social miscalculation. *Hrafnkell's Saga*, for instance, describes how a man lost his chieftaincy through inattention to his following and regained it by carefully building it anew. In chapter 117 of *Njáll's Saga*, when one man urges Flosi to kill Njáll and his sons for vengeance, Flosi responds:

"I see it clearly that though our wish be granted that we kill Njáll or his sons, then they are such significant people and highborn that there will be such an aftermath that we will have to go in front of many people's knees and ask others to help before we arrive at a settlement and out of this difficulty. You may also assume that there will be many stripped who before have much wealth and some will lose both their wealth and their life."

Wealth was accumulated and lost in social stratagems rather than by means of commerce. The sagas relate many incidents of people gaining wealth by marriage and force, even by poetry, but rarely by trade. The important luxury goods whose consumption or distribution was necessary to social manipulation came from overseas.

The system of reciprocal relationships entailed in the chieftain-follower and chieftain-chieftain relationships, here as in other such systems, is related to the consumption of display objects that indicate the ability of a person to enter reciprocal relationships. Hence the central importance of the goods of chiefly consumption.

Many of these goods did not originate in Iceland; and early on, there was not sufficient wool to gain them by exchange with Norwegians. One source of means of exchange was by raiding and pillaging abroad, standard episodes in most of the family sagas.

As the number of sheep increased, available wool and woolen goods increased. The major use for wool was for exchange. Sheep were needed for meat and wool, but to provide as much meat as people needed they produced more than enough wool. Those with much land, labor, and hay had many sheep (hence, much wool) and could engage in foreign exchange; but, as Gelsinger (1981: 153) points out, since all of them had more than sufficient woolen goods, woolen goods were not very useful for exchange within Iceland. Better-off Icelanders could use such means of ex-

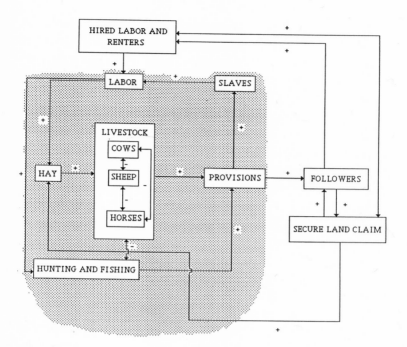

*Figure 3. Dynamics of production in medieval Iceland.*

change to acquire some of the foreign goods necessary for social maneuvering (Durrenberger 1988a).

Figure 3 illustrates the relationships among the elements of the system of production and how these relate to political variables, which in this system were inseparable from economic ones.

Initially there were probably large household units, like Skalla-Grímur's, with its own internal redistributive system reminiscent of those Marshall Sahlins (1958) describes in Polynesia, to take advantage of ecological diversity. More land meant more hay, more livestock, more provisions; more slaves meant more labor, more hay, and more hunting and fishing. Labor requirements were not constant through the year. They peaked at hay-making time and again shortly after at roundup time. During the winter, labor was only useful for feeding livestock and perhaps for hunting and fishing. If a household maintained enough slaves for haying, it had to use its resources to feed them through the winter, when they contributed less to the household.

When some people began to offer to work for others, as in *Hrafnkell's Saga*, it was less costly to use their labor and to free slaves. Landowners could take in laborers for peak periods and let them fend for themselves at other times. Provisions translated into followers, necessary to secure claims to land upon which the whole system rested. The more followers, the more secure the claim to land, the more seasonal labor and renters were available, the more hay, and so on. Large households were dispersed and we would expect an explosion of small households, each dependent on a large landowner for part of its subsistence through seasonal labor or rental arrangements.

*Eyrbyggja Saga* illustrates several dimensions of this dynamic. The sons of Þorbrandur free two slaves who are brothers, Úlfar and Örlygur. They operate their own farms. Chapter 30 tells us that Úlfar is a hardworking farmer, good at getting in his hay and lucky in livestock raising so that his animals do not die from disease. Þórólfur, father of the chieftain Arnkell, takes some of Úlfar's hay. Arnkell tells his father to repay Úlfar, but Þórólfur says that Úlfar is already too well off for a slave. Arnkell pays for the hay.

In Chapter 31 Þórólfur threatens Úlfar, so Úlfar enters into a partnership with Arnkell, making his property over to the chieftain in return for protection. The Þorbrandssons are irritated at this because they think the land of their ex-slave should belong to them, not to someone else. Here they are operating on the logic of one extended household, while Úlfar and Arnkell are operating on the logic of independent households.

When Örlygur dies, Úlfar claims his land as his brother and heir, but the Þorbrandssons claim it as the ex-masters of the ex-slave. Arnkell backs Úlfar's claim. The sons of Þorbrandur try to get the support of Snorri the chieftain. Þórólfur has Úlfar killed, the sons of Þorbrandur claim Úlfar's property, and Arnkell maintains his claim to the property. When the sons of Þorbrandur appeal to Snorri, he tells them that Arnkell will control the property because he is stronger than they are. Meanwhile Snorri and Arnkell fall out over other matters; in chapter 37 Snorri and the sons of Þorbrandur agree to cooperate to kill Arnkell, which they do.

These episodes point out the contradiction between the idea of one large household of many parts like Skalla-Grímur's and a set of detached households each dependent on a central one, like those of Blund-Ketill and his renters or Hrafnkell and his hirelings. It also suggests the importance of maintaining a following and coalition relations with other powerful people to maintain claims to land.

Thomas McGovern et al. (1985) argue that ecological processes paralleled social-political ones. With archaeological data, they show that the land was fully in use between the years 1000 and 1100 and that pressure on pasture and woodland resulted in environmental degradation. Small and medium-sized farmers were most likely to suffer in bad years, and more so in a second or third in close succession. After two or three bad years out of five, such farmers would cease to be independent and would join the ranks of seasonal workers, renters, or impoverished wanderers of the countryside. As the cooling of the little ice age set in about 1200, bad years were frequent and contributed to the increasing availability of seasonal workers and renters and the impulse for large landholders to expand their holdings. Many potential tenants were available and the turnover rate was high, so detailed meadow-by-meadow knowledge of particular places declined. Landowners were more involved in social and political maneuvering than in farm management.

Gelsinger (1981) suggests that no group of professional merchants developed in Iceland because those who had the wherewithal to exchange for foreign goods—wealthy landowners and chieftains—could not abandon the management of their estates, entourages, and alliances, lest they lose their tenuous claim to their land. They could have delegated either management of their estates or their foreign trips to kinsmen, friends, or hirelings. That they did not in any great numbers is due less to a conflict of management responsibilities between the two functions than to the fact that there was no market exchange in Iceland. Icelanders did not develop the institutions or the cultural conventions consistent with markets and market exchange, the sine qua non of merchants.

Large landowners with plentiful labor could amass stores of woolens, take them abroad, and bring back imported goods, but the only use for such goods was in social-political maneuvering, not as capital. All they could hope to gain from using wealth as capital was more woolen goods, pointless to those who already had more than sufficient wares (Gelsinger 1981; Durrenberger, Durrenberger, and Eysteinsson 1988).

These households operated in terms of the logic of household economies everywhere (Durrenberger 1984a, 1988b). There was a definite, though not linear, relationship between the needs of the household and its production. We would therefore expect to see a relationship between a measure of total production and the number of consumer units in the household, the major source of demand. This relationship would vary by class. Chiefly or wealthy households would be more involved in foreign exchanges, and we would expect evidence of greater woolen production or perhaps the production of dried fish for exchange (Amorosi 1989). It is possible that off-site disposal of fish might have been to other places in Iceland either as part of a redistributive system such as Skalla-Grímur's or as part of an exchange system among members of a coalition of chieftains. Reciprocal exchange was central in either case.

# 3. CHIEFLY CONSUMPTION

arcel Mauss opens his classic essay on *The Gift* with a lengthy quotation from *Hávamál*, the speech or matters of the high one, ancient aphorisms about the conduct of life collected and recorded during the mid-thirteenth century in Iceland. Among the passages he quotes (1967:xiv) on gift giving are:

> Friends should rejoice each other's hearts with gifts of weapons and raiment, that is clear from one's own experience. That friendship lasts longest—if there is a chance of its being a success—in which friends both give and receive gifts.

> Know—if you have a friend in whom you have sure confidence and wish to make use of him, you ought to exchange ideas and gifts with him and go to see him often.

> Generous and bold men have the best time in life and never foster troubles. But the coward is apprehensive of everything and a miser is always groaning over his gifts.

We are used to thinking of consumption as driving production and distribution in capitalist economic systems (Henry 1963). Mauss was concerned with societies in which neither the general realm of the economic nor the specific aspect of consumption had been separated from other aspects of life, but in which there were "total acts," each with aspects which we in a more differentiated society might label religious, economic, political, or social. To use Karl Polanyi's aphorism (1944:57), the economic is embedded in the social.

During Commonwealth Iceland, political processes provided much of the impetus for consumption of goods beyond basic subsistence needs, that vast realm of consumption needs which Karl Marx relegates to historical and moral determination (1977: 275). In this subarctic herding economy, meat and milk products from sheep and cattle were major subsistence goods along with the fruits of the hunt at sea and on land. There was limited use for quantities of woolen goods. Because wool could be converted into foreign luxury goods, it gained exchange value apart from its limited use value. It replaced silver as a medium of exchange and for the calculation of exchange equivalencies among other goods. It came to be a standard for purchase, inheritance, dowry, and legal awards. To make an analogy with modern times we might say that woolen goods circulated like paper money, but the value was based not on gold, silver, or the promises of governments, but on the potential for conversion into foreign luxury goods. These goods, obtained in various ways, especially from Norway, were in demand among the chiefly class. It is the source of this demand, the uses of these goods, that I examine here. First, a few examples.

Major items of chiefly consumption were fine clothes; grain for brewing in connection with feasts; wood for houses and, later, churches; and weaponry. None of these was available in Iceland. Before Gissur Þorvaldsson succeeded in unifying the chieftains of Iceland in 1264, his enemies attacked him and burned his establishment at Flugumýri. He escaped, though many of his allies and kinsfolk perished. Chapter 174 of the *Saga of the Icelanders*, one of the contemporary sagas, catalogues the losses:

> At Flugumýri burned much wealth which many people who were there owned and many people had loaned their valuables there, down bed-clothes and other valuables, and it all burned. But the greatest wealth that burned belonged to Gissur, first the farm at Flugumýri, which had no equal in splendidness in Skagafjörður except the see at Hólar. All of the buildings were elaborately worked, the front hall all paneled going to the main room, the hall and main room were all hung with tapestries. There also burned many valuables which Ingibjörg, Snorri's daughter, owned.

In *Eyrbyggja Saga* (chap. 13), about 200 years earlier, Snorri the chieftain, later to develop a reputation for craftiness, is young and returning from Norway.

And when they prepared to leave the ship, the Breiðafjörður people, there was a great difference in the outfits of Snorri and Þorleifur Kimbi. Þorleifur bought the best horse he could get. He also had a very splendid colored saddle. He was outfitted with a sword and a gold-inlaid spear, a very gilded dark blue shield, all his clothes were elaborately worked [of high quality, handsomely made]. He had also used almost all of his trading goods for them. But Snorri was in a black cape and rode a good black mare. He had an old trough-saddle and his weapons were little embellished. . . . people ridiculed his outfit a lot. Börkur took it that he had been unlucky with his wealth, as all was spent.

Snorri will inherit from Börkur but wants to claim the farm at Helgafell immediately. Börkur offers to buy Snorri out. Snorri replies that Börkur can set the price, and let Snorri decide who will buy whom out. Börkur agrees and sets a price on the farm, but stipulates that Snorri must pay the full amount immediately without going into debt. Snorri agrees. In chapter 14 Snorri pays the money and has as much left over. Börkur says, "Your silver has become more ample, kinsman, than I thought." Börkur's expectations of Snorri are based on his appearance, a cultural convention Snorri knows well enough to turn to his own advantage to trick his uncle.

Þorkell, Guðrún Ósvífur's daughter's fourth husband, lives at Helgafell, which Guðrún acquired from Snorri. In chapter 74 of *Laxdæla Saga* he dreams that his beard is so big that it spreads over all of Breiðafjörður. He interprets this to mean that his power and authority will extend over the whole of the district. His wife suggests it could mean that he will fall into the bay of that name. That summer Þorkell goes to Norway to get timber for a church. King Ólafur receives him well with gifts of silver and a cloak as well as timber. In the spring, when the timber is being loaded into Þorkell's ship, the king goes out for a morning walk and sees a man climbing on the large church he is having built. It is Þorkell Eyjólfsson measuring all components of the church. Þorkell explains he plans to duplicate the church in Iceland. King Ólafur suggests he cut a yard from every beam and the church will still be the biggest one ever built in Iceland. Þorkell says the king can keep his wood if he wants, but Þorkell will not reduce any dimensions because he can get wood elsewhere. The king says it is presumptuous for a landowner's son to compete with the king, that he does not begrudge him timber, that the church could never be big enough to hold all his conceit, and he prophesies that Þorkell will get no use from the timber. Þorkell returns to Iceland.

Chapter 74 of *Laxdæla Saga* explicates the proper uses of wealth:

Now Þorkell sits home at his farm in the winter. He had a Yule-drinking at Helgafell, and there was a great crowd. And with all he had great magnificence that winter and Guðrún did not hold back from it and said that wealth was to consume, so people could aggrandize themselves and it should also be displayed. . . .

This is precisely the function I am suggesting for all of the items of chiefly consumption. Before he could build the church, Þorkell drowned in the bay of which he had dreamed.

When the Icelandic sagas spend a few lines describing a weapon or a person's dress, it is an important sociological statement not simply for literary impact. From a person's dress and weapons we learn what he or she has to offer in the way of support and whether it might be worthwhile to make a social investment of some wealth to make an alliance.

Chapter 32 of *Njáll's Saga* tells us that Gunnar's brother, Kolskeggur, urges him to ride to the Alþing after they return from abroad. "Your honor will grow, because many will turn to you there." "I have little mind," says Gunnar, "to boast, but I like to meet good people."

Chapter 33 opens:

Gunnar and all rode to assembly. And when they had come to assembly, they were so well dressed that there was no one there who was equally well dressed, and people went out of every booth to be amazed at them. . . . Many people went to meet Gunnar. . . .

It was one day when Gunnar walked from Law Rock; he walked down past the Mosfell booth. Then he saw women walking toward him and they were well dressed. It was the one in front who was best dressed. . . . She was named Hallgerður. . . .

These two well-dressed people get married and have many adventures together until Gunnar gets killed. The point here is the importance of their fine clothes for social calculation. The same judgments are entailed in houses, horses, trappings, weapons, feasts, and gifts.

Mutual support, gift giving, visiting, and feasting were major components of coalition relationships. When a chieftain wanted to initiate such a relationship with another, it was typically by an invitation to visit or feast, an offer of support, or a gift. One of the surest signs of friendship was mutual feasting, in which each party feasted the other on alternate years, as Gunnar and Njáll do in *Njáll's Saga* (chap. 35). If two people attend or sponsor different feasts on the same occasion at households close to each other as Gísli and his brother Þórkell do in *Gísli's Saga* (chap. 15), it is a sure sign of enmity. The "feasting" unit is the same as the "support" unit, though it may not be very stable. It is for this reason that the sagas often record in detail who attended what feasts and how they were arranged. Such accounts indicate how the alliances were aligned at a moment.

To be a chieftain, one had to be able to sponsor such feasts with enough drink brewed from grain to keep people in a festive mood for some days at a time. One had to be able to offer support and to deliver it. Hence, one had to have a sound entourage. Without an entourage, a chieftain's friendship was meaningless. A chieftain had to be able to support and protect his followers. If he could not or did not, there was no reason to belong to his entourage. In *Njáll's Saga*, the chieftain Mörður falls on hard times when his followers abandon him. When his father, Valgarður the gray, returns from abroad, he chastises him for the way he has managed the family's chieftaincy; Mörður explains that people have been withdrawing their allegiance from him and giving it to Höskuldur. Valgarður then says he wants his son to repay Njáll's family by dividing them by slander to make Njáll's sons kill their foster brother, Höskuldur, and hence drag them to their own destruction.

William Miller (1983) shows how the killing of Höskuldur is a political act. As in any such system, whether a Melanesian big-man system or a Thai entourage, the largest of the "center man," "big man," "patron," or chieftain provides the coherence for the group. In the Icelandic, as in other social systems, people must be able to make accurate predictions about how others can and will react to events. One indication of chieftains' ability to provide support to followers or other chieftains was their observable level of consumption of wealth. This was the central point of Snorri's trick by misdirection.

The fineness of his house, clothes, weapons, horses, and trappings all were indicators of a chieftain's ability to offer support, to concentrate significant force for his own purposes and those of his friends and followers.

Chieftains consumed such goods as timber for houses and churches, grain for brewing, and imported weapons and clothing to support their friends and followers and to indicate, by the level of their generosity and consumption, their ability to support others (Durrenberger 1976). These functions are integral aspects of the institution of chieftaincy, which persisted from the first settlement until 1264. The context for the functioning of this institution changed over the course of time (Durrenberger 1985). The watershed period seems to be about the year 1000, when seasonal labor became available.

With this less costly source of labor, large landholders began to expand their holdings. Whereas chieftains had gone overseas to obtain luxury goods in the early part of the Commonwealth, few did in the later period. It was more important to stay in Iceland to manage the entourages and coalitions necessary to insure enough force to maintain claims to landownership on which the extraction of value rested. At the same time, and for the same reasons, the necessity for foreign goods increased. For a while, Norwegian traders came to Iceland.

At the end of the twelfth century, prices for imports to Iceland became quite high because of scarcity in Norway and because alternate sources of wool had developed in Europe. The exchange value of Icelandic wool, the only major export product, dropped relative to grain and other foreign products. There was an overabundance of woolens in Iceland and a scarcity of grain (Gelsinger 1981: 162). In 1192 there was a famine and 2,400 people died of hunger and disease (Gelsinger 1981: 8). The Norwegian trade diminished because the traders had no use for Icelandic wool and had no grain to sell. The climate began to grow cooler in 1200, with longer winters and shorter summers.

By this time there were no slaves or freed slaves. There were people who owned land and those who did not. Among those who did not were some who rented land from landowners under various types of arrangements and those who tried to subsist on seasonal work. There was also a category of homeless poor who wandered from place to place with no fixed means of subsistence.

Those who had access to sufficient resources to support a household were legally defined as tax-paying farmers, *bændur*. Each of them had to be a follower of a chieftain from his own quarter. Chieftains were dependent on farmers for support—to feed their increasingly large personal followings or armies, to support them at assemblies, to accompany them on raids on other chieftains or their followers, and to defend them from such raids. Without such support and the ability to amass force, claims to ownership of land, which defined the class system as well as the forms of appropriation, had no force. Farmers had to rely on some chieftain to be able to defend their claims to property, though this might lead in the end to the loss of the property. Chieftains had to rely on farmers to enforce their followers' claims and their own as well as to expand their territories into others' and to defend themselves.

By definition, each farmer (*bóndi*) represented a unit of household production, and his main interest in the political system was to maintain that status. As chieftains strove to expand their power, their demands on their followers became heavier. The farmers wanted to live to cut another field of hay or shear another flock of sheep and to collect their rents from their tenants.

Chieftains' increasing demands for demonstrations of force in support of claims to ownership conflicted with the subsistence demands, the economic roles, of farmers. Chieftains sometimes used coercion to insure support. In spite of this contradiction, farmers had to rely on some chieftain in order to maintain their claims to land.

Relations between chieftains and farmers were not smooth. Chieftains had their "own" estates to support their establishments, and some maintained followings of armed men, but this was a difficult proposition, since it added consumers to the household without adding production (Durrenberger 1980). The chieftains had to rely on their followings of farmers to support them with both arms and supplies. This was one component of any farmer's household fund, his "rent" so to speak (Wolf 1966), expenditures for travel and support for the chieftain, without which his chieftain or another would take his land and livestock. In addition, expeditions took labor from the farm and put the farmer's life at risk. Even so, a farmer's claims to land were not secure, since his chieftain might abandon him, another more powerful chieftain might claim his land or simply take it, or a farmer might lose his land in a realignment of alliances among chieftains, which were frequent.

Support of chieftains, even if their support in return was dubious, was one of the conditions for heading an independent household. Dependent people—renters, cotters, and others—went with the household head. It was as close as one could come to a secure claim to land, and failure to provide support for chieftains was costly.

Independent householders appropriated the labor of the class of dependent renters and seasonal workers. The chieftain class, who based their claims on hereditary privilege and attempted to back them with force, appropriated the products and labor of householders in turn. They sometimes met overwhelming force from other chieftains.

Each chieftain had to attempt to muster overwhelming force. It was therefore not possible to maintain any balance of power among chieftains. In order to gain overwhelming force, each chieftain had to expand—and on an island such as Iceland, with limited resources, any expansion was at the cost of other chieftains. Such attempts at expansion on behalf of all the chieftains provided much of the dramatic action of the Sturlung period.

The alternative to expansion was to lose influence, the ability to make good one's claims, one's followers, and one's power as a chieftain. Each chieftain had to expand his influence or cease being a chieftain. The resources for expansion came from the householders' funds, from the production they appropriated from the landless workers as they replaced slaves. The "social cost" of the system was the creation and maintenance of a large class of poor and landless people.

In these conditions the institution of chieftaincy became exaggerated and the demand for luxury goods increased just when the foreign trade was falling off and the Norwegian traders came less and less frequently.

There were increasing levels of violence and decreasing security during the Sturlung period. Both factors were results of the drive to expand landholdings, and both reinforced the institution of chieftaincy through competition until the surviving chieftains were more powerful and more voracious, and the need and thirst for luxury consumption goods increased in pace, as we would expect.

The problem was that at just this time Norwegian traders found the trip to Iceland increasingly profitless (Gelsinger 1981). There was no market economy in Iceland (Miller 1986a). The exchange values of goods against one another and standard exchange values were negotiated at quarter assemblies for each quarter and at the Alþing for the entire island (Gelsinger 1981: 35–44).

Wealth was accumulated and lost in social maneuvering, not through trade. Consumption of luxury goods was one component of this social maneuvering, and that depended on relations with Norway.

When they came to Iceland, Norwegian traders had to be skilled diplomats (see Sahlins 1972: 303) to conduct their trade and return alive. They had to find someone to stay with, some chieftain who would support them while they were in Iceland, because they could not make a return trip until the next summer. They often fell afoul of some Icelander before they could get back to Norway.

As the exchange value of Icelandic wool fell relative to European goods, Icelanders attempted to redefine it by action of the price-setting assemblies (Gelsinger 1981: 164–175). The Norwegian traders did not honor these tables of exchange values, and there were a number of misunderstandings between Norwegian traders and Icelanders until it became dangerous for Norwegian traders to go to Iceland and more likely that they would lose rather than gain wealth. For these economic and cultural-political reasons, they stopped coming to Iceland, and the sources of chiefly consumption goods dried up just when consumption was being highly emphasized by the concentrations of chiefly power in fewer hands.

The archaeologists Thomas McGovern, Gerald Bigelow, and Daniel Russell (1985) document increasing pressure on pasture and woodland which had widespread and intense impact, resulting in environmental degradation. They go on to ask why people skilled in subarctic farming would persist in "practices that produced neither riches nor stability for the community as a whole" (1985: 20).

The small and medium-sized farmers who were most likely to suffer losses in a bad year would lose the critical balance of resources necessary to be defined as independent households after two or three bad years out of five. Small and middle-sized farmers would cease to be independent and would join the ranks of seasonal workers, renters, or impoverished wanderers of the countryside. The cooling of the little ice age starting about 1200 made bad years frequent and contributed to the increasing availability of seasonal workers and renters and the impulse for large landholders to expand their holdings. Many potential tenants were available and the turnover rate was high, with the consequent deterioration of management practices as the distance between ownership and farm management increased. As McGovern et al. say (1985: 263):

. . . impoverishment of smaller gothar [chieftains] and former freeholding thingmen [followers] would actually directly strengthen the great chieftains both economically and politically. In the bloody turmoil at the end of the Commonwealth, short term payoffs may have been all that mattered to the leadership of the day, and the early warnings of Little Ice Age and progressive environmental degradation may have been heard only by the politically powerless.

When the ceiling on the size of holdings was removed by the availability of seasonal labor about 1000, large landholders began to expand their holdings. There was no state to guarantee differential access to resources, but the system of appropriation of wealth was based on concepts of property. Thus, individuals had to enforce their own claims to ownership by force. As they began to expand their holdings, these claims more and more frequently clashed and force was more frequently used.

As the use of force increased, so did the necessity to maintain overwhelming force and the necessity to build and maintain entourages and coalitions through the social maneuvering that was facilitated by the consumption, gift giving, and display of imported goods. With high turnover rates of tenants and the distancing of ownership from management, local knowledge of conditions deteriorated and, with it, the ecological basis of the grazing economy.

Icelanders stayed home to tend to their feuds; Norwegians began supplying exotic goods in trade for wool. When wool lost its value in Europe, the Norwegians were less welcome in Iceland, though their goods were in even more demand. Because of loss of profitability of the trade and increased dangers, Norwegians more or less stopped coming to Iceland.

When Gissur Þorvaldsson got the chieftains to agree to cede their authority to the king of Norway in 1264, the Icelanders demanded that the Norwegians send trading ships to Iceland in return. To get the luxury goods they needed the chieftains had to give up being chieftains and the fundamental contradiction of stratification without a state. Unwilling to relinquish stratification, they were absorbed into a state system.

# 4. POLITICS

L ate in the ninth century chieftains left Norway and the British Isles with their families, followers, and slaves to settle in Iceland. They claimed land and portioned it out to their followers and friends. Although a number of their relatives came to Iceland, they dispersed on the island and the kindred never developed as a kinship group (Phillpotts 1913).

The *Book of Settlements* records that some took their land from others by force. The question arises why, in a context of freely available land, the original settlers did not elect the option, outlined by Morton Fried (1967), of developing an egalitarian society with equal access to land. The main settlers were wealthy chieftains. They had no inclination toward egalitarianism. The *Book of Settlements* records that the Irish slaves of an early settler, Hjörleifur, the brother of Ingólfur Arnarson, the first "official" settler, killed him and went to the Westman Islands with the livestock and women of the household. Ingólfur went to the island and killed them all. One does not have to credit the story or the source to believe that, in spite of plentiful land, it was not available to all. This is the important sociological, as opposed to historical, conclusion. As this example shows, there could be severe consequences for those who attempted to violate the social conventions of claiming land. The facts that there were slaves and that chieftains could appropriate land and then give it to others indicate that there was unequal access to basic resources, the defining characteristic of stratified societies (Fried 1967).

The principles of ownership of land and slaves were central from time of the settlement, and there were local assemblies based on Norwegian models. The elite of such a society must somehow cope with its fundamental contradiction: to maintain privileged

differential access to basic resources without institutions to enforce or protect this axiom of social stratification. Commonwealth
chieftains attempted to do this by establishing a General Assembly, the Alþing, a legislative and juridical body, in 930.

From early on, there were local assemblies. Each chieftain
(*goði*) was obliged to attend annual meetings of the General Assembly where law was made and changed and cases were adjudicated according to intricate procedures.

When the chieftains established the Alþing they also adopted a
code of law. Lawspeakers were appointed for three-year terms.
Their function was to recite the law orally, one-third at each meeting of the General Assembly, so that the full code would be recited
within the term of each lawspeaker. The lawspeaker had the
power to change the law, for if no one else reminded him of any
item that he omitted to recite, it was dropped from the code.

Even though a complex system of courts evolved during the next
decades, most disputes were not adjudicated (Jones 1935: 21).
Violence was an important "dispute-processing mode and . . .
outcomes reached by talk, although not rare, were neither easy to
achieve, nor desired by most disputants" (Miller 1984: 100).
Plaintiffs had to enforce legal judgments by holding courts of execution at the farms of the defendants. These often led to violent
clashes. The Alþing was not primarily a legal institution but an
arena for building coalitions, for making, breaking, and testing
connections.

The social system rested on concepts of property, of unequal
access to resources, but there was no state to defend claims to
ownership. One could maintain such claims only through coalitions of force which depended on being a member in good stand-
ing in some chiefly entourage or developing some personal power
base for oneself by trying to head an entourage. Being a member
or leader of an entourage was primarily a matter of social maneuvering, generosity to one's following, arranging good marriages
and foster relationships, holding feasts, winning important law
cases at the Alþing, and winning fights.

Those who were not chieftains had to select some chieftain to
follow. Relationships among chieftains were equally voluntary.
There were two sorts of groups: the entourage of a chieftain and

the coalition of chieftains. Both shifted and changed membership through time. Parties to either kind of relationship had to see some advantage to maintaining it. Kinship played very little role (Rich 1976), and sagas (e.g., *Víga-Glúmur's Saga, Gísli's Saga, Laxdæla Saga*) detail feud relationships among members of what would be bilateral kindreds, had they existed (Phillpotts 1913).

There were probably thirty-six chieftains. Chieftainship was defined as a kind of property, as power, but not wealth. It could be divided, sold, inherited, or assigned to others for various periods.

As in other such systems of hierarchic entourage relationships, there are no egalitarian relationships. Authority rests on the assumption that the one in authority is a benefactor to the subordinate. Authority goes to the provider of benefits in hierarchic relationships. The greater the resources one has, the more reciprocal relationships one can form and the more enduring the relationships are. Entourage heads try to cultivate as many reciprocal relations as their resources allow. Lucian Hanks's (1972: 86) description of Thai entourages fits equally well in the Icelandic Commonwealth: "The poor manager fails to balance membership with resources, while the good manager gains and holds his members. But let him not be niggardly, for the man who fails to use his resources wholeheartedly for his followers may find himself as shunned as if he were bankrupt."

About 960 Iceland was divided into four quarters. Each quarter, except the northern, had three assembly districts, each with three chieftains. The northern quarter had four assembly districts. Now people had to select a chieftain from within their own quarter, and an assembly site was named for each district. Cases had to be heard in the disputants' assembly or, if they were from different assembly districts, in the quarter court at the meeting of the Alþing. Unanimity was required for judgments. Cases that could not be resolved in quarter courts were referred to a fifth court (established about 1004) where a simple majority of judges could decide a case. Not all local assemblies functioned, and some were consolidated into others (Jóhannesson 1974: 238).

Of this complex legal organization, and the need for agreed-upon rules, Peter Foote (1963: 96–97) says, "Widespread knowledge of the law and widespread active participation in legal procedure must have been a stabilizing social influence in its encouragement of respect for law and legal form." There were thirteen assemblies. Each had a judicial court of thirty-six judges, twelve appointed by each of the three chieftains from among his followers. These courts were charged with hearing disputes. Thirty of the judges had to agree on a decision that accorded with law (Jones 1935: 15). There were 468 nonchieftains who were conversant enough with the law code at any one time to sit in such courts. Gwyn Jones (1935: 17) discusses "the presence of a large and influential body of unofficial lawmen in Iceland who made it their business to memorize the laws. . . ." Because of their relatively short terms of office, the lives of past and future lawspeakers overlapped with the life of any person in the office. Thus, Kirsten Hastrup's (1985: 206–207) conclusion that "until the laws were written down (which process began in 1117–18), the lawspeaker was (theoretically, at least) the only person to know the entire body of laws" is incorrect.

It is difficult to assess "respect" for the law in any practical terms, but it is certain that the code recorded in *Grágás* was widely violated during the Sturlung period and before in terms of the basic principles of organization and procedure it laid down. Not all local assemblies functioned. Chieftains did not always attend the General Assembly as the law required. *Grágás* specified that one individual could not manage more than one chieftaincy, but many in fact did (Jóhannesson 1974: 237). Jón Jóhannesson (1974: 230) summarizes cases which were not conducted according to the procedures specified in law, some by Snorri Sturluson while he was lawspeaker. If the lawspeaker himself as well as chieftains could violate basic tenets of procedure, such as holding procedures in an assembly in which the defendant was not a resident, we can only guess at the force of the law code in regulating the behavior or determining the thoughts of others. It is certainly incorrect to suppose that *Grágás* was a charter for medieval Icelandic thought or practice as Hastrup (1985) does.

The most significant aspect of this system from its inception is that redress was left to the individual who won the case. Courts of execution were held to confiscate the property of people who were outlawed. These were often vigorously resisted.

While the system seems conceptually rather neat, it was not very tidy in practice. Peter Foote (1963:104) says that "vengeance was sanctioned most fully against a man who had been outlawed by the courts, but in many cases feuds never got to the thing, or reached no conclusion there if they did, and the system was worked out in private." Of 520 cases of feud recounted in the Icelandic family sagas, fewer than a tenth (50) came to any legal settlement. More than half were handled by private actions of vengeance (297), a fifth were settled by agreement (104), and another tenth started as legal procedures but were arbitrated or settled by agreement (60). Nine were legal cases that could not be concluded (Jones 1935: 21).

An example from the second half of the twelfth century is instructive. It is from *Sturlunga Saga*, the *Saga of Hvammur-Sturla*, which was written between 1200 and 1225 about the father of the Sturlungs, including Snorri Sturluson. Einar and Sturla, who are chieftains of the same area, are involved in a series of disputes. Chapter 9 tells us that both of them take their cases to court with wide support. Each presents his case so well that both Sturla and Einar are sentenced to lesser outlawry only.

After the assembly they both collected followers for the court of execution and Einar went to Hvammur with three hundred and fifty men but he left behind . . . a hundred men.

Sturla rode west to Saurbær with sixty men . . . and held a court of execution at Staðarhóll and then rode to Hvammur. But Einar's group sat by the road. . . . And Einar jumped up and urged an attack but Þorleifur sourpuss asked him not to call the men into such great danger as they could never escape as was to be expected if such a great crowd should fight. And many good men came forward with him to take part and the men separated there without mishap.

Chapter 10 begins, "Both now remained outlaws that winter. But in summer they both prepared to ride to assembly." On the way, Einar turns back and rides with a group of men to Hvammur:

And when they came to Hvammur they brought all the people into the church and plundered all the wealth and burned the farm and took everything west to Saurbær and . . . Einar then rode to the assembly with ninety men.

And when people came to meet Sturla and told him the news, he said Einar had without doubt maintained a fire [fired] flawlessly for a whole [one] night.

Einar and Sturla agree to let a bishop arbitrate the case. He stipulates that Einar should pay sixty hundreds for the raid, but Sturla is to pay fifty hundreds for offenses against Einar, and Einar is to repay the robbery. At Sturla's request, the bishop swears an oath that he has arbitrated the case equitably.

Then people went home from the assembly and were nominally reconciled. The pillaging was mostly righted but not altogether.

Sturla had his farm built in the summer and before winter nights it was no worse than before.

Needless to say, this was not the end of their disputes, but it suggests the difference between the apparent neatness of the system and the divergence in practice. It was not unknown for people forcibly to disrupt courts in which their cases were going badly. Jones (1935: 19) sums up the situation:

. . . everything depended on the power of the litigant, for whom legal procedure was a means of putting to trial not his rights but his strength. The stronger party always gained the day, and we may define Icelandic legal procedure as little more than legalized lawlessness. Icelandic law was a paradox. The righteous could not be upheld, nor the unrighteous brought to book, save by the employment of those lawless private means, superior skill at arms or greater numerical strength, with which the law should have dispensed. . . .

There were chieftains, there was law, there were concepts of property, but there was no constituted authority—legal decisions of courts only added weight to personal solutions. Law or no, courts or no, decisions or no, one could do just as much as one's influence, cunning, and power at arms allowed. For cases brought to local assemblies or the General Assembly, contemporary sagas as well as many family sagas record the figures of arms, men, and who supported whom with what force rather than details of arguments and decisions. In the *Saga of Hvammur-Sturla* and the *Saga of the Icelanders*, the results of cases are reported but nothing of the process except the strength of each side. Clearly the saga-men saw that the armed power each side of a case mustered was more significant than any niceties of procedure or argument. There was no state. It was just this aspect of Commonwealth that made it attractive to the chieftain-settlers and that they perpetuated as long as they could.

In a state, a ruling class maintains its position through its monopoly of violence, which it exercises through formal and specialized social forms (Fried 1967: 231).

As Morton Fried (1967) has pointed out, a stratified society without a state is one of the most unstable of social forms. Although he does not mention the Icelandic Commonwealth, his speculations on the fate of such a society could stand as a thumbnail sketch of the Sturlung period. The hallmark of stratified societies is unequal access to resources. Fried argues that the people who are denied access to resources would assert principles of equal access and instate egalitarian or rank forms of organization, or that those who claim privileged access would institute state forms of control to insure their continued enjoyment of disproportionate shares of resources. It may take some centuries, as it did in Iceland, but ultimately, "the stratified society will face a magnitude of internal disputes, pressures, conflicts," and if "there is a partially congruent kin-organized system of restraints and balances, it is doomed to increasing incidence of failure if relied on to maintain the political integration of the society" (Fried 1967: 225).

Many confrontations between chieftains have the indeterminate result of the meeting between Hvammur-Sturla and Einar after they have outlawed each other. There are threats and bluster, and each chieftain has many followers. Each tries to intimidate the other, but some "good men" try to reconcile them or at least prevent a pitched battle in which many people will get hurt or die. Such attempts are often successful when the forces are more or less evenly matched, and less so when one side enjoys overwhelming superiority of force.

Chieftains were not beyond using coercion to insure support, as the following incident relates. A chieftain, Kolbeinn the young, is recruiting followers. In chapter 130 of the *Saga of the Icelanders*, he leaves his main force with "only" a hundred men and rides to ask a farmer named Hálfdan to support him. Hálfdan refuses. Kolbeinn has him and his brother driven into the main room of the house with their servants. Then:

> Kolbeinn was there during the night with all the group and had all their weapons and horses taken from the brothers.
>
> After that he sends word to Hálfdan's brothers that they should stand up with him or else he said he would go around wrecking all the district for them. The four brothers Björn, Andrés, Haraldur, Filippus stood up with all the forces they could gather.

In spite of this contradiction, farmers had to rely on some chieftain in order to maintain their claims to land. While the inheritance customs codified in *Grágás* seem quite orderly in Kirsten Hastrup's (1985) analysis, inheritance of land is often hotly disputed in the *Saga of the Icelanders*. One who wanted another's land could often find a third party with some inheritance claim and acquire the claim to legitimize taking the land.

There was a ruling class, but the law was not an instrument with the force of a state to insure its privileged position against other classes. The chieftains did this individually by the force of their coalitions and followings. While the law specified more or less tidy rules for inheritance, sale, and other transfers of property, there were no state institutions to give it practical meaning. Law had only the currency of the force of arms backing any particular interpretation. It could only be used for the framing of rhetoric of justification for acts of force.

Chapter 79 of the *Saga of the Icelanders* relates the practices of Sturla Sighvatsson (grandson of Hvammur-Sturla mentioned earlier) with respect to property:

> Sturla then went to Dýrafjörður, from there to Arnarfjörður and to Álftamýr. Sturla demanded to purchase Álftamýr from Bjarni Sverrisson for Odd Álason, but Bjarni did not want to sell. Sturla's men demanded to buy a good fur cloak from Bjarni. He also did not want to sell it. But then the cloak disappeared and Bjarni charged Sturla's men. They abused him in return. When the cloak was not found, Sturla went and abused

them. Then it came out that Bjarni had caused the cloak to be lost. Sturla
became so angry that he wanted to have Bjarni killed. Then people took
part, and it came out that Sturla took the land at the value he quoted.
Then Sturla went home south to become both well off for wealth and
repute.

Óraekja, son of Snorri Sturluson, another of Hvammur-Sturla's
grandsons, supported his personal retainers mainly by letting
them pillage whatever they wanted wherever they were. Such incidents are too numerous to list, but some involve more than mere
pillaging or murder.

Chapter 132 of the *Saga of the Icelanders* tells us that in the
summer Gissur had Dugfus Þorleifsson's establishment in Selvá-
gur at Strandir seized and all the livestock taken. After that, his
men had no provisions and the farmers had to provide for them.

Such victims had recourse to the law if they could find a chieftain to support them. The saga tells of few such instances and
normally records that the individual was killed or where he went
in exile. One example from Hvammur-Sturla's time, the latter half
of the twelfth century, is instructive. Chapter 28 of his saga tells
that Birningur Steinarsson and his wife, Helga Þorgeir's daughter, had a daughter named Sigríður. The couple did not get on
well with each other and were divorced. Each remarried and had
children. Birningur married Guðbjörg Álf's daughter and they
had a son named Þorleikur. Birningur named Þorleikur as his
heir, but the daughter of his previous marriage, Sigríður, "came
off badly." Sturla and Einar Þorgilsson were still at odds, as they
were for the rest of their lives. Einar claimed that Birningur's marriage to Guðbjörg was not lawful, so Þorleikur could not inherit.
He claimed that Sigríður was the rightful heir and purchased
from her her expectations to inherit. The saga continues:

Then Einar demanded that Birningur go home with him with his
[Birningur's] wealth and Einar said he would arrange something for Guðbjörg and her son [Þorleikur], such as he would decide. But Birningur did
not want that. He then lived at Heinaberg and had much wealth.

And in autumn Einar sent his house servants out to the heath to collect
Birningur's geldings [castrated male sheep] together. They went and

herded home to Staðarhóll seventy geldings and Einar had all slaughtered.

Then Birningur went to Hvammur and met with Sturla and sought his advice and said he wanted to transfer all of his wealth to Snorri, and it was decided that Birningur went to Hvammur and was there while he lived and Guðbjörg maintained the farm at Heinaberg.

And this case closed so that Sturla did not prosecute Einar for the pillaging, nor did Einar say his disagreement to Birningur's transfer to Snorri, and each sat there with what they had got.

Einar had bought an inheritance claim from Birningur's disinherited daughter. Birningur had given the estate to Sturla in return for protection against Einar, but Birningur's wife, Guðbjörg, managed the estate. We can follow the story some years later, after Sturla's death, when Þorleikur, the son of Birningur and Guðbjörg, was about twenty. While the event seemed closed, chapter 2 of the *Saga of the Icelanders* tells us that shortly after Sturla died Einar claimed Birningur's property from Guðbjörg. She rejected the demand. Einar and his men then tried to drive away the livestock.

The women of the household chased the cattle away from the attackers, but Guðbjörg held onto Einar's cape while her son and foster son attacked him. Einar's men rushed to him, but the boys and woman got away. After a time Einar died of the wounds he received. One of his kinsmen asked Jón Loftsson, the most respected man in Iceland at that time, to help him with the case. Jón, chapter 3 of the saga tells us, replied: "But it seems to me matters have become hopeless if it shall not be righted when no-account men kill an aristocrat and I want to promise you my support in this case when it comes to assembly."

Einar Ól. Sveinsson (1953: 43) takes this as evidence of chiefly arrogance which was not very widespread. Sturla's faction defended the two at the assembly and paid "a great deal of" money to reach a settlement. Einar's killers were sentenced to outlawry and given money to get out of Iceland.

In summary, a chieftain wants the land of a farmer and concocts a spurious inheritance claim to get it. The farmer gives his farm to a competing chieftain in return for protection. When the protecting chieftain dies, the other one reasserts his claim. The sons of the farmer, defending their land and stock, injure the chieftain, who dies of his wounds. The farmer's sons are outlawed and have to leave Iceland.

Claims of inheritance were only worth as much as the armed support behind them. This follows from the fact that claims to ownership, property, were only worth as much as the armed support behind them. This meant that to assert any claim to ownership, whether by inheritance or any other means, one had to back the claim with armed force. Chieftains were focal points for concentrating force to protect and to forward claims to property. Chapter 102 of the *Saga of the Icelanders* tells of Hvammur-Sturla's son, Snorri:

> When summer was almost over Snorri Sturluson sent word to Órækja his son that he should come there to the south with a crowd and Snorri wants to go to those northlanders who sat in his farms. Órækja collected followers around all the West Fjords and had up to four hundred men and went to the southern districts.

Chapter 15 of the *Saga of the Icelanders* relates:

> Bersi the wealthy priest expired in the same year as Bishop Brandur. Snorri Sturluson took his inheritance after him. He then moved his farm to Borg and lived there several winters.
>
> Þórður Böðvarsson, his mother's brother, then lived at Garðar and had followers up around Akranes and many up around the district. It seemed to Þórður Böðvarsson that his sister's son Þórður Sturluson put the followers closest to Þórður Böðvarsson under himself. Þórður Böðvarsson then gave Snorri half of the Lund-men's chieftaincy and he should keep the followers safe from Þórður Sturluson and other aggressors. But when Snorri had taken over the followers, then it seemed to Þórður Böðvarsson that he was more aggressive toward his friends than his brother Þórður had been before.

We have seen the kind of coercion chieftains used to gain support when farmers were reluctant. Such cases are common in the *Saga of the Icelanders*. In chapter 95, Kolbeinn the young was living at Flugumýri with a large force of men. His friendship with Sighvatur, another chieftain, son of Hvammur-Sturla, brother of Snorri, had fallen off. Many prominent farmers of his area were friends of Sighvatur. Kolbeinn heard that the farmers were not likely to follow him if he came into conflict with Sighvatur. Kolbeinn hid in a house while another farmer talked to one of the farmers who was partial to Sighvatur, Jón Markússon, and learned that what he had heard was true. Kolbeinn ran up from the cellar with curses and said that Jón deserved to be slain. Kolbeinn's followers ran into the room, but Jón escaped with his life because he was a priest.

Kolbeinn then accused another of his farmers, Kálfur Guttormsson, of planning an attack on his life, which Kálfur denied, though he admitted to being a friend of Sighvatur's. He agreed to accompany Kolbeinn on any expedition in which four other specific farmers, including Hallur of Glaumbaer and Önundur Þorgrímsson, would participate. When Kolbeinn was gathering forces to attack Sighvatur and had between two and three hundred, he sent men to demand that Kálfur go too. When he was riding past the farm, he told Kálfur to join him, as Hallur and Önundur were with him. Kálfur refused. When Kolbeinn discovered that Sighvatur had learned of his attack, he turned back. Kolbeinn decided to kill Kálfur and went to his farm in the afternoon.

Before they arrived, Ósk, the mistress of the house, had asked Kálfur whether he wanted dairy products or dried fish to eat. Kálfur answered that he would declare himself in the fellowship of the Apostle Peter because he could no longer put his trust in the chieftains of this world.

Kolbeinn and his men entered the house, prevented Kálfur from getting his axe, and led him and his son outside. Kálfur asked for a priest, and Kolbeinn provided one to hear his confession, and had him and his son killed. Then the chieftain demanded that the farmers supply everything for his homestead and his ally Óraekja, Sighvatur's brother's (Snorri's) son.

Large landholders began to expand their holdings. There had been burnings, betrayals, and mutilations before, but the violence of the Sturlung period was unique in its ferocity, frequency, and intensity. The *Saga of Þórður kakali*, one of the Sturlunga sagas, tells us that in June of 1244 Þórður and Kolbeinn fought from their ships. Þórður lost after inflicting heavy casualties on Kolbeinn's forces. Þórður put ashore and stole all of the available horses for his wounded to escape on. The able-bodied could walk to the hills. He had the ships' fittings stripped and stored, along with those men who were wounded so badly they could not travel, in a church for sanctuary.

After a rest to count the dead and wounded, Kolbeinn went after Þórður and said that if he could not meet him to fight it out, ". . . then shall we sail to the West Fjords and harry, burn farms, and kill people and so waste the habitations that Þórður may not oftener grow strong from there for war against us."

Kolbeinn followed Þórður, pillaged the church, killed one of the wounded, and, for the first time in Iceland, used the modern method of warfare of depriving his enemy of access to subsistence resources.

After that, Kolbeinn had all [Þórður's] ships taken and had some with him but some he had burned. On this trip that was done, which never before had been done in Iceland. He had taken some of the whales, but in some he had fires set and burned up, said that Þórður would not feed himself on them or his men to war on him. Kolbeinn then robbed all Strandir and sailed from there to the West Fjords and said they should be totally laid to waste so that Þórður might not grow strong for war from there.

# 5. EXCHANGE

Bruce Gelsinger (1981) discusses Icelandic foreign commerce as though it were governed by market relationships, and there is little doubt that relationships of supply and demand, which varied through time with different goods, had a part in determining their exchange values. At local assemblies and the Alþing Icelanders prepared lists of various goods and their exchange values relative to one another to govern exchange either for the island as a whole or for the local assembly district for which the list was drawn up (Gelsinger 1981: 33–44). That drawing up such lists of exchange values was a matter for assemblies suggests that there was no price-setting market. Had there been a price-setting market, such lists would not have been necessary, nor would they have been tolerated (Miller 1986a).

One of the uses of tables of equivalent values would have been to reach settlements in which wealth had to be exchanged, such as those mentioned above, when so many hundreds were awarded to a claimant. Transfers of wealth via legal awards were facilitated by such equivalencies. These equivalencies were not set by the invisible hand of the market, but by the public debate of assemblies, a social rather than an economic process.

It is no surprise that the rates of exchange themselves were set by the social process of negotiation at the assemblies rather than by a price-setting market. The law, as recorded in the law book *Grágás*, specifies maximum returns for labor, interest rates, and that when there are divisions or transfers of property, including land, a group of neighbors must set values on the property. This does not suggest they were followed, but that it made sense to specify such relationships. In a society in which values are set by markets, there would have been no necessity for such provisions or lists of exchange values of various goods against others, since they could be established by market functions. In the Icelandic Commonwealth, any attempt to put exchange on such an impersonal footing as a market would be antisocial.

Exchange was largely a matter of reciprocity within entourages, involving a chieftain and his followers. The sum of reciprocal relations was a redistributive system with the chieftain at the center receiving wealth from one source to disperse it to another. His function as a lender, a usurer, was in the context of entourage building and maintenance—it was not an economic function as we know it in state societies.

Chieftains were voracious enough, but they relied on building followings, coalitions, and alliances and translated the power these gave them into force either at assemblies to influence legal decisions or in fighting. As an aspect of this social maneuvering to gain power, they rented land, loaned wealth, and traded with Norway, both taking goods to Norway and welcoming Norwegian traders into their followings. But this was not conceived of as being the same kind of activity as peddling, lending, and maneuvering with wealth to gain wealth. Rather, it was the transformation of wealth to support, support to force, and force to wealth. Investments were in people, not goods, even in the foreign trade. It was social rather than economic maneuvering.

Trade and usury were not in themselves objectionable activities. In *Njáll's Saga*, two people who are described as influential, respected, and popular engage in lending and collect interest. Njáll and Hrútur are both held up as exemplary figures. Usury itself is not condemned, but rather usury for the antisocial purpose of wealth accumulation. Njáll and Hrútur use their wealth for social ends, to cement ties of affinity and friendship, to build followings.

There is scant mention of internal trade in the sagas, but there are clear indications, and this is true for the contemporary sagas as well as the family sagas, that people who attempted to accumulate wealth without using it for social purposes were scorned. Einar Ól. Sveinsson (1953: 47) interprets incidents from the *Saga of the Icelanders* to suggest that "such men were unpopular with the common people, and the chieftains coveted their wealth and had no scruples in trying to lay their hands on it." The most plausible reason for the rare mention of internal trade is that it was considered a natural part of the whole sphere of social exchange and reciprocity and did not exist as a separate category.

The Icelandic nonmarket economy, then, was grounded in the workings and values of reciprocity within entourages and coalitions, in hierarchic reciprocity, and in socially determined exchange. The "economy," therefore, was integral to the various aspects of social interaction and hence to concepts of kinship, marriage, fosterage, friendship, relationships with neighboring farmers, and alliance with chieftains and other farmers. A chieftain's wealth was of no use if it could not be used to ensure popularity and a large following.

The satire of *Bandamanna Saga* derives its force from the juxtaposition of hereditary prestige with lack of sufficient wealth or goodwill to enact the generosity appropriate to chiefly status. Chieftains are engaged not in conflicts of honor but in coercion to line their own pockets. The process of law is not a just forum for adjudication but a corruptible and self-serving procedure.

As Sverrir Tómasson (1977) points out, Ófeigur is described as being like a chieftain except that he lacks the title and wealth. Lacking wealth does not distinguish him from the chieftains of this saga; his appropriate use of that wealth does. For much of the saga he is also lacking in the appropriate dress and bearing although, in this respect, he develops in an interesting way. After placing him genealogically, chapter 1 continues: "He was a generous man in everything, but wealth management was not easy for him, he had much land, but less movable property. He did not spare food for anyone, even though there were many provisions which the household needed to have."

The saga follows his son, Oddur, for a while to show that getting wealth seems as easy for him as it is difficult for his father before reintroducing Ófeigur humorously described in rags at the assembly in chapter 5. For a person of Ófeigur's position to totter about in rags is just as incongruous as to describe aristocrats as poor. Ófeigur repeatedly plays on such poverty:

Ófeigur said: "Then let a somewhat fat money-bag come into the hands of this old man, because the eyes of many people happen to be money-squinting." (chap. 5)

Sometimes Ófeigur lowers the money-bag down from under his cape and sometimes pulls it up. He finds that they run their eyes to the money-bag. (chap. 6)

These eight men talk. Styrmir and Þórarinn tell about the state of the case and where it had got to and how much Oddur's fortune was worth, and that all would become very wealthy. (chap. 7)

This is made explicit in the insults of chapter 10: Ófeigur describes each of the chieftains with the unchieftainly characteristics of vanity, pride, overbearingness, injustice, ignorance, greed, or poverty. Similarly, reciprocity (and the ability to offer it) is the central dimension of Egill's upbraiding of Hermundur and of Styrmir and of Hermundur's response.

The reason for the concern with the issue of reciprocity in *Bandamanna Saga* relates to the conditions in the thirteenth century when it was written. Sverrir Tómasson (1977) agrees with Gunnar Karlsson (1977) that this saga is about a power struggle between the old order of chieftains (*goðar*) and the newly rich aristocrats (*höfðingjar*) whose economic foundation was the wealth of the church farms and tithe taxes. As Tómasson (1977: 110) puts it, "In *Bandamanna Saga* it is simply shown that a fat money-bag may break all bonds." The humor of the saga points to the difference of orientation between those who gain wealth in order to disperse it socially and those who gain it for private or antisocial use. Egill charges Hermundur with the ultimate form of private use, hoarding buried treasure where no one can find it (Durrenberger and Wilcox 1990).

This theme is reminiscent of *Hen-Þórir's Saga*, which values the old paradigm of social economy and despises the logic of commerce (Durrenberger, Durrenberger, and Eysteinsson 1988). The difference is that, while Hænsa-Þórir operates only in market terms rather than in terms of the current social logic, Oddur uses his wealth socially to purchase a chieftainship, support his followers, and at the end, as Tómasson (1977: 108) puts it, "with the marriage of Oddur and Gellir's daughter capital lies down with inherited power in the same bed."

Much of the humor of *Bandamanna Saga* centers on the themes of wealth and reciprocity. Except for Oddur, the wealthy are stingy, and the poor are generous. This suggests these must have been salient dimensions of the social order of the saga writer. Stinginess and reciprocity of help are central in the exchange between Egill and Hermundur:

Hermundur answers: "You are lying, Egill, as you did in winter, when you had gone home after I had invited you home from your wretched house for Yule, and you were glad of it, as was to be expected. And when Christmas was over, then you became sad, but when I saw that, I invited you to stay there with another person, and you accepted and were glad. But in spring, after Easter, when you went home to Borg, you said that thirty winter-grazing horses had died on me and all had been eaten."

Egill answers: "I don't think that it is possible to exaggerate your stinginess, but I think either few or none of them were eaten. But all people know that I and my people are never short of food, though my wealth-management is not always easy, but the circumstances at your house are such that you had better not say anything about that." (chap. 10)

Egill draws a similar contrast between himself and Styrmir.

. . . we are unlike each other, each promises others help, and I give it, when I can, and do not spare it, but you run when spearshafts are raised. It is also true that farming is difficult for me, but I'm not sparing with food to any person, but you are food-grudging. . . . It befits me, that my householders have it hard when there is nothing, but it befits them worse who starve your household, when nothing is lacking. . . .

The family sagas make many references to trading trips, both of Icelanders to Norway and of Norwegians to Iceland. There is no doubt that the trade was of great economic importance (Gelsinger 1981). Marshall Sahlins stresses the diplomatic content of long-distance trade in primitive societies: there is a "facility of a translation from trading goods to trading blows" (1972: 302). The acquisition of foreign goods may be urgent, but with no sovereign power there must be some way to secure peace by extending sociable relations to foreigners. Thus, trading partners usually establish friendship or quasi-kinship relationships. Sociability requires reciprocity, and the best strategy is "a generous return relative to what has been received, of which there can be no complaints" (Sahlins 1972: 303). Partners tend to overreciprocate.

If the trade with the Norwegians had involved a great deal of conflict, it would have ceased early on. While the Norwegians and the Icelanders were clearly not always operating in terms of the same sets of assumptions, one might say that they operated quite well in terms of common "misunderstandings" (Durrenberger 1975). While the Norwegians were marketing·their goods, the Icelanders were carrying on an exchange on their own terms, whereby a group of three chieftains determined the price of the goods. As long as the Norwegians were satisfied with the prices, the trading would run smoothly enough. There are numerous examples in the sagas of how the Icelanders did not treat the Norwegians as mainly traders, but as individuals with whom to establish social relationships. Norwegians accommodated themselves easily to the situation in Iceland, offering support and generosity for local support and a place to stay.

However, there were some conflicts, as illustrated in *Hen-Þórir's Saga* and in the contemporary *Sturlunga Saga* collection. One would expect such conflicts to have increased in the last century of the Commonwealth, because by then there was less demand for Icelandic woolen goods, as other countries developed weaving industries based on their own domestic wool supplies, and because there was less grain available in Norway due to worsening climate and increasing population. When the relative values of wool and grain began to shift in Norway, as Gelsinger (1981) documents, the merchants were in a bad position. From their point of view, the old equivalences of grain with woolen goods were no longer validated by the economic facts of market exchange in Europe, but this made no sense to the reciprocity-oriented Icelanders.

Such is the context for a scene in chapter 15 of the *Saga of the Icelanders*. Snorri Sturluson, the famous chieftain and writer, housed a skipper of a ship from the Orkneys over the winter, although they did not get along well. Snorri had some of the skipper's meal taken and said that he would determine the price for it, in spite of the skipper's insistence that he name his own price for it. Although he later managed to take revenge by killing one of Snorri's men, the scene illustrates the power over trade that their social positions granted Icelandic chieftains, a power that barred any kind of bargaining or mutual settlement concerning prices.

This privileged trading status of the chieftains was supposed to rest on a concept of reciprocity, and the closing chapter of the *Saga of Guðmundur dýri* (in the *Sturlunga Saga* collection) expresses this concept forcefully and symbolically. Some Norwegian merchants cut off the hand of a relative of the chieftain Guðmundur. Guðmundur stipulates that they pay thirty hundreds as compensation. They find that too much, and eventually he grants them another offer, the ultimate and "ideal" act of reciprocity:

Guðmundur said: "I will make you another offer, that I will pay Skæringur the thirty hundreds . . . and I will choose a man from your followers, someone who seems to me the equal of Skæringur, and chop off his hand, and you compensate him as little as you want."

But the Easterners [Norwegians] did not want that and paid up the wealth and Guðmundur took Skæringur with him from the ship.

While Guðmundur's offer to exchange a hand for hand may illustrate the tenacity of traditional social reciprocity in Iceland, it also exemplifies the boundaries and imminent exhaustion of that paradigm. The saga was written at a time when the Commonwealth was collapsing under the strain of tensions from within and without. The family sagas were also written during that tumultuous period, and it is unlikely that they escaped the effects of changes that the society was undergoing. *Hen-Þórir's Saga* is a good example of how the family sagas grew out of the conflict between models of social exchange and market exchange.

Hen-Þórir's actions run counter to the traditional mode of socioeconomic exchange. Þórir's wealth comes directly and exclusively from trade and he does not build any kind of reciprocal network around it. But in the absence of any state apparatus, there is no institutional framework which will protect such one-sided internal trade. Nor is it upheld through kinship ties. Significantly, the saga gives no genealogy for Hen-Þórir and he appears to have no relevant kinship or affinal connections.

Wealth can be used to get support, even in the absence of a following or kinship ties. In this saga there is symmetry between the use of wealth (market model) and the use of affinal relationships (social exchange model) to muster support. Both are used to create immediately useful connections. Affinal ties are made parallel with money, and the sagaman obviously favors the former.

Hen-Þórir decides to seek a relationship with one of the chieftains of the district, Arngrímur, by offering to foster his son, Helgi. It is generally a man of lower social status or prestige who offers fosterage to another. This is the first time we see Hen-Þórir appealing to the model of social exchange, in which fosterage is one of the central means of establishing or strengthening reciprocal social relationships.

After Arngrímur rejects his offer, Hen-Þórir offers him half of his wealth in return, and Arngrímur does not turn down such an excellent offer. Just as in Thailand and other hierarchic systems of patron-client relationships, followings and support depend on wealth. A chieftain could not overlook sources of wealth that would enhance his ability to attract followers and support. When Þórir offers Arngrímur and Þorvaldur wealth in return for support, they do not decline.

For Hen-Þórir, this fosterage is just another market item, not a reciprocal relationship of mutual support. He "buys" Helgi from Arngrímur, and therewith Arngrímur's support should he need protection for his market endeavors. We are told that Arngrímur's support did indeed prove beneficial to Hen-Þórir, and his investment is worth the high price because he can now count on the chieftain to support his economic claims against his debtors when he tries to collect.

Here we see the ambiguity and ambivalence of the two models of exchange and proper conduct. Hen-Þórir's market mentality, which aims to secure his investments by a further economic investment, contrasts with the older model of social transaction.

We are clearly witnessing an attempt at marketization of the Commonwealth economy. Buying support is generally not well looked upon in the sagas. In *Njáll's Saga*, the means by which the opponents Kári and Flosi muster support for the crucial assembly at the Alþing contrast sharply. While the heroic Kári seeks support only through friendship and social ties, Flosi, the burner, offers monetary reward to some people in order to increase his following. The contrast is again stressed in the way the two groups recruit their legal advisors. Flosi pays his. The upright Njáll gives his advice to Gunnar as a part of their mutual bond of friendship and support, while the villainous Mörður *sells* his advice to Gunnar's enemies. Acquiring social support through purely pecuniary means introduces a foreign element into the system, which unpredictably offsets the tenuous balance preserved through the reciprocal socioeconomic system.

In Commonwealth Iceland, a system of extraction based on claims to ownership of property, on concepts of the unproblematic differential access to resources in favor of a chieftainly class, and on the unwillingness of those chieftains to subordinate themselves to state institutions to protect their privileged positions entailed the contradiction of an economic system based on property relationships without a congruent institutional system to enforce them, stratification without a state. Ownership was as sound as the force one could muster to defend it. There was a complex system of law, but it was only so many rhetorical labyrinths in the face of the stark realities of the decisions by power which in fact prevailed. As slavery diminished and claimants to land enlarged their holdings by using seasonal labor and tenancy arrangements to work them, they had to enlarge their circle of power by enlarging their entourages.

At the same time, a new stress was put on the old system of recruitment of support through social and economic maneuvering. The relations with Norwegian traders, who operated in terms of a market paradigm, became more and more problematic, and an internal trade in Iceland began to develop. In addition to the contradiction of property without a state, a model of market exchange developed in contrast to social exchange. It was conceivable to purchase and sell support and social relations as though they were commodities, a term that was foreign to this nonmarket economy.

This was the social and economic context of thirteenth-century Iceland, before the chieftains bowed to the inevitabilities of their inequitable social order and subordinated themselves to the hegemonic power of Norway. In this stateless but stratified society, extraction depended on entourages and economic maneuvering was social maneuvering. There were no price-setting markets, and attempts to gain wealth by accumulating merchant or usurer's capital were considered antisocial. In the saga of Hen-Þórir we see high value placed on entourage building with affinal relations and nothing but scorn for Þórir, who is despised because he follows a commercial rather than a social logic. These values derive from the social and political structure of the period and shape the sagaman's construction of the saga, the way he handles genealogies, descriptions of character, and even the narrative structure (Durrenberger, Durrenberger, and Eysteinsson 1988).

# 6. KINSHIP, CHURCH, AND KING

I t is impossible to read far in *Sturlunga Saga* without encountering references to kinship and the church, as the examples cited above indicate. The chiefly families were focal points for wealth and power. Einar Ól. Sveinsson (1953: 46) suggests that Órækja was such a marauder because his father, Snorri, failed to set him up properly as a chieftain. Even with meager personal fortunes, such as Snorri had when he came of age, a chiefly family was sufficient to provide the nucleus of power and wealth to build from by recruiting a following by whatever means, whether by advantageous marriages, intimidation, or conquest. However, kinship connections themselves did not count for much, as the relations among the sons and grandsons of Hvammur-Sturla indicate. There were continual attacks among brothers, between uncles and nephews, and even between fathers and sons. Family connections did not provide allies or support in themselves.

Much has been written about the cultural, economic, and political impact of Christianity in Iceland. I will not attempt to review the literature here. It is clear that churchly office was in the same practical category as chieftaincy. The chieftains selected the bishops and shared the tithe taxes with them. It has often been suggested that control of church lands, hence access to tithes, was an important means for concentrating wealth in the Sturlung period. However, the church offices were the same as chiefly office. The church simply expanded the number of competing chieftains. The bishops and clerics were not any meek servants of the Church of Rome in this period. They feuded, sponsored suits, mediated, had followings, made alliances, intimidated, fought, and killed in the same way as secular chieftains.

Access to church lands and tithes did not change any principle of wealth concentration or its direction. It was simply another means, like the manipulation of inheritance claims, that the powerful or aspiring could use to gain more wealth and power. This did not become a difference, a matter of a new focus of wealth and power, until after the absorption of Iceland into the Norwegian polity, when there was a serious attempt to institute a separate church and state law. Kirsten Hastrup (1985) documents the increasing influence of the clergy on the formulation of the law from the time the Alþing decided to record it in 1117 until 1253, when the Alþing decreed that where there was a conflict between the law and "God's law" the latter should obtain. From the evidence presented above, it should be abundantly clear that it made no practical difference where the law came from or who formulated it or what its content was. The law did not count. To suggest that the church gained influence through the law is therefore fallacious.

I will not deal here with the controversial question of the cultural impact of Christianity and its possible influences on the formation of the literature of the period (see Durrenberger 1985). In terms of the practical conduct of affairs, the influence of Christianity on the laws was nullified by the slight influence of any form of law. The institution of church lands and the tithe law offered alternate means to achieve what the aristocratic class had until then been doing by other means. While these may have altered the rhetoric of justification, they did not affect the political and economic realities of the age. That leaves the possibility of an ideological impact of Christianity. In light of the behavior of officers of the church, this would be difficult to demonstrate. One of many examples will suffice to show that excommunication was not even an effective weapon.

The *Saga of the Icelanders* tells that the chieftain Kolbeinn Tumason ruled in the north. He appointed Guðmundur Arason to be the bishop of the north when Bishop Brandur died. Guðmundur was Kolbeinn's wife's cousin. Many people commented that Kolbeinn had wanted Guðmundur chosen bishop because he thought he himself would thus control both laymen and clergy in the north. If this was his expectation, he was disappointed, and quarrels soon developed between the two. Kolbeinn prosecuted one of Guðmundur's priests. The bishop forbade the proceedings, but the priest was sentenced. Kolbeinn made an expedition against the bishop and summoned all of his house for outlawry. The farmers urged Kolbeinn to let the bishop arbitrate the case and to pay any fines he should decide. When the bishop announced the fine, Kolbeinn paid half and said the farmers should pay the other half. The bishop instigated lawsuits against two chieftains who had maimed and mutilated a man they had taken from the monastery and who had forced a great deal of money from a farmer. Kolbeinn and the other two chieftains forbade all buying and selling with the bishopric. The bishop excommunicated Kolbeinn, but neither Kolbeinn nor his followers paid any attention. In the spring, Kolbeinn rode to the bishopric and summoned all of the bishop's homemen, priests, deacons, and laymen to be tried for outlawry.

The bishop, in his robes, and his men were positioned up on the house to defend it. The bishop read out the sentence of excommunication in Icelandic so that they would understand it. Chapter 20 of the saga comments that if Kolbeinn had been less restrained on that occasion there would have been a battle.

Kolbeinn recited a mocking poem about excommunication instead and left. The suits continued, and the bishop excommunicated Kolbeinn again. Kolbeinn had succeeded in getting a number of the bishop's men outlawed and held a court of execution at the see. The bishop disregarded the outlaw status of the men and allowed them to attend church. Kolbeinn and all the men the bishop had excommunicated also attended church.

The priests associated freely in religious services and in other affairs with those whom the bishop had excommunicated. Although the bishop forbade them to do so, they continued to celebrate Mass. He excommunicated them for their disobedience.

Kolbeinn attacked the bishop to get the outlawed men from him. Thus began a series of battles in which the bishop figured. The significant point in this context is that his acts of excommunication were not effective even against priests.

As Morton Fried (1967) suggests, the kinship system offered no restraint. Nor did the church alter the political and economic picture. Various chieftains had tried to gain paramount power in Iceland, among them, Sighvatur and Snorri. The one who succeeded was Gissur Þorvaldsson, who had Snorri assassinated. He was not without opposition—his enemies attacked him repeatedly—but he did succeed, as an earl of the king of Norway.

The manipulations of the Norwegian kings have also been mentioned as reasons for the fall of the Commonwealth. As with the church, the king could provide alternate rhetorics of justification, could give Icelanders titles, hold chieftaincies, and arbitrate disputes between chieftains. But this itself did not affect the everyday practical political and economic realities in Iceland any more than the reformulation of the law under the influence of Christianity did. The Commonwealth fell not because of Christianity or the king of Norway, not for reasons of any decay in values or cultural changes, but because of the practical contradictions entailed in a stratified society without a state.

# 7. IDEOLOGY

Among thirteenth-century Icelanders, as among the contemporary stateless Lisu (Durrenberger 1989), Cheyenne (Lewellyn and Hoebel 1941: 94), Nuer (Evans-Pritchard 1940), and other stateless people the quest for honor was a quest for reputation, the need to be well spoken of and evaluated by others (Bauman 1986: 142).

Richard Bauman stresses the performance aspect of honor and argues that *drengskapur* (honor) rested on the public display and acknowledgment of valued behaviors; hence, it was "a performance domain par excellence, characterized by the display of signs of moral worth before an audience with conspicuous attention to good form in the pursuit of honor and reputation" (Bauman 1986: 143). Bauman reinforces E. V. Gordon's view that conduct was evaluated not in moral but aesthetic terms: "The heroes and heroines themselves had the aesthetic view of conduct; it was their chief guide . . ." (Gordon 1981: xxxiii).

Altercations provided the substance for performance, and fellow Icelanders were the audience. A rich record of such cultural displays has come down to us in the form of the Icelandic family sagas. We do not know who wrote the sagas. Some of the authors may have been Christian clerics, but others surely were not (Tómasson 1977). What we do know of the sagas is that they are thirteenth-century interpretations of tenth- and eleventh-century life in Iceland. We can ask how such interpretations can inform our understandings of the social and political realities of either period as well as why they were written and how we can interpret the events they relate as cultural artifacts.

The latter question points to a cultural exegesis, an explanation of concepts of causality, category, value, means, ends, and relationship to make the events intelligible to us as they would have been to their original audience. This is a classic goal of anthropology. To understand why this set of ideas held sway we must understand the political economy of the period and its dynamics, another classic goal of anthropology. By watching this process for a period of about four hundred years, we can appreciate the dynamic interactions among cultural ideologies, social and political arrangements, and events.

Ari Þorgilsson lived from 1068 to 1148. A priest, he wrote the *Book of Icelanders*, a chronicle of events and people from the first settlement in 874 to 1120. He mentioned the names of his informants and that he selected them for their clearness of mind, good memories, and relationship to the events, much as Lewellyn and Hoebel (1941) assessed their sources for accounts of Cheyenne trouble cases. Ari recorded that in 1117 the General Assembly decided to revise and record the laws at the house of Hafliði Másson according to what Bergþór, the lawspeaker (responsible for memorizing and reciting the body of law), and other knowledgeable men agreed was law. They would announce the law the next summer and would keep those which were not opposed by a majority. This lawbook has not survived. There were several written versions of law, because *Grágás* specifies that what is found in books is to be taken as law. If the books differ, then the books of the bishops are to be preferred. If their books differ, then the longer would prevail. If both were equally long and differed, then the book at Skálholt would be used. It specified that everything in Hafliði's book would be accepted unless it had been modified since (Stein-Wilkeshuis 1986).

It is impossible to say how much of this book is represented in *Grágás*. *Grágás* has been preserved in two manuscripts which date to about 1260 and 1280. It is not possible to assign dates to individual provisions within it. The provenance of the manuscripts is unknown and neither is an official compilation (Miller 1990: 42).

If we credit any of the other sources for the period, or the internal evidence of the lawbook itself, it is clear that some of the laws recorded in *Grágás* were obsolete, some never enacted, and some unenforced (Dennis et al. 1980; Miller 1990: 231). This poses the problem of how to interpret this document.

Kirsten Hastrup (1985) has used *Grágás* and nineteenth- and twentieth-century Danish commentaries on it as inspiration for the construction of models of medieval Icelandic systems of thought about time, place, and kinship. Karl Lewellyn and E. Adamson Hoebel (1941: 25–26) suggest that modern jurisprudence and Icelandic sagas teach the same lesson: "that even when such rules are known and clear in words, one still does not know the legal system save as he studies case after case in which the rules have . . . been challenged or broken." Observing that Hastrup's (1985) treatment of medieval Icelandic culture is innocent of so-cial fact because she largely ignores the evidence of social practice presented in the sagas, Miller (1986b, 1990) advocates a case ap-proach to medieval Icelandic law based on saga evidence.

A major problem is that saga scholars have often projected the categories and values of state societies unreflectively onto medie-val Iceland (Durrenberger 1985; Durrenberger and Durrenberger 1986). While most anthropologists would agree with Miller that it is fruitless to isolate accounts of law from depictions of social life, a law code inscribed by the people themselves should reflect something important about their culture. It should echo their ba-sic assumptions and values, a dimension of *Grágás* that Hastrup (1985) appreciated, but did not adequately explore.

One of the advantages of an anthropological approach is the light comparative studies can shed. By observing a series of forms from different areas of the world, we see that the variation is lim-ited and that certain features accompany others wherever they oc-cur. For instance, there are a limited number of political forms regularly associated with a limited number of forms of exchange and production (Fried 1967). One frequently mentioned dimen-sion of law in stateless societies is that it is analogous to civil law in state societies; there is no public law, only private law. This suggests a radically different view of law and rights between state and stateless societies and indicates some of the problems of pro-jecting state-based conceptual structures onto stateless societies such as medieval Iceland.

Bronislaw Malinowski (1934: xxv) observes that "the primitive family, village and kinship groups are not subject to courts of law, to policemen, to codes, to judges, or public prosecutors. And yet the laws are kept—to a large extent." He poses the question of why people who live in stateless societies with no institutions to force them to comply with laws follow their customs or laws. If we take the perspective advocated by Morton Fried (1967), we might well reverse the question and ask why there is such apparent order in societies based on the principle of unequal access to resources, societies in which the majority work to support a minority who do not.

This order seemed so natural to European social scientists that they took it for granted as the standard against which to measure other societies. This is implicit in our terminology when we speak of "stateless" societies as though "state" societies were the default or unmarked reference point. Every state invests considerable resources in schools, rituals, information control, and other forms to shape the imaginations of its citizens to accept the state as inevitable and natural, "the way things are done," rather than one social form among many (Hobshawn 1983a, 1983b). For modern state dwellers, the social and political forms of the state are not problematic but natural. When confronted with the literature of a nonstate society, then, they have little alternative but to interpret it as a familiar state literature and in so doing to project their own cultural and social categories onto an alien literature as the saga scholars have done. Anthropology, perhaps especially the anthropology of law, points out that the state is neither a universal form nor natural. It is one historical form of social organization.

A. R. Radcliffe-Brown distinguished between public delicts, transgressions of customary rules which are treated as a threat to society at large, and private delicts, breaches of custom which are treated as limited transgressions against individuals or against small groups within the society (Leach 1977). Edmond Leach (1977: 24) argues that, while in England murder and theft are public and sexual violations and violations of contract are private, in many societies it is the opposite:

For example, wherever we encounter the institution of *feud vengeance* (and in the simpler societies that is the norm rather than otherwise) the crux of the matter is that homicide and theft are classed as private debts. The offence, whether intentional or accidental, provokes direct reprisal by the relatives of the injured party.

Others may insist that the feuding parties resort to arbitration, but the function of the arbitrator is simply to restore peace, not to adjudicate the rights and wrongs of the conflict or inflict penalties. Decisions must be acceptable to both sides—the arbitrator has no means by which to impose a verdict by force (Evans-Pritchard 1940; Leach 1977). So it was in medieval Iceland.

Paul Bohannan indicates that Tiv do not distinguish between wrongs which injure the entire community and those which injure individuals. "The distinction which Europeans draw is a folk distinction. The distinction which I have drawn between *kwaghbo, kwaghdang* and *ifer* is a folk distinction. We can compare the two sets of distinctions. But it is just as wrong and just as uncomprehending to cram Tiv cases into the categories of the European folk distinctions as it would be to cram European cases into Tiv folk distinctions" (Bohannan 1957: 120).

To obtain their rights and justified claims on others, to make other people perform their obligations, Tiv have recourse to three sorts of self-help: jural institutions in which one must do one's own detective and police work and enforce the decisions of the court, direct action, and reprisal which must equal the offense "to even out the score" (Bohannan 1957: 137–138).

Tiv, therefore, use both the institutions of self-help and *jir* [jural institutions] to enforce their rights. This is not, however, the way they put it. Their emphasis is on means of making others carry out their obligations. They discuss social acts by comparing them with what one "ought" to do or to have done. Both the *jir* and the institutions of self-help are used for the same purpose, that of making people carry out their obligations towards one. (Bohannan 1957: 131)

E. E. Evans-Pritchard speaks only of civil law among Nuer, "for there do not seem to be any actions considered injurious to the whole community and punished by it" (1940: 168). To get a settlement, one must use force. "The club and the spear are the sanctions of rights" (Evans-Pritchard 1940: 169). Fear that the injured man and his kin may resort to violence is the main motivation for paying compensation. His cause can be just, but if from a weak lineage he is unlikely to receive compensation. A strong kin group will not support a cause they find unjust (Evans-Pritchard 1940: 171). Nuer have a keen sense of personal dignity and rights. "The notion of right, *cuong*, is strong. It is recognised that a man ought to obtain redress for certain wrongs."

"It is the knowledge that a Nuer is brave and will stand up against aggression and enforce his rights by club and spear that, ensures respect for person and property" (Evans-Pritchard 1940: 171). "A man must stand up for himself against any encroachment on his person and property. This means that he must always be prepared to fight, and his willingness and ability to do so are the only protection of his integrity as a free and independent person . . ." (Evans-Pritchard 1940: 184).

Though it may be manifested in different ways in different circumstances, Bronislaw Malinowski argues that reciprocity is the basis of all culturally defined behavior.

What the anthropologist recognises as a body of customary law is simply a set of specifications of rights and duties between the individual members of a social system. If we refuse to fulfil our obligations towards others we must anticipate that others will refuse to fulfil their obligations toward us. This, from Malinowski's point of view, was the supreme sanction which leads to general conformity. (Leach 1977: 14)

On Ontong Java there were many connections of mutual obligation: husband and wife for food; fishing group on one another; fishermen on those with specialized knowledge of navigation; members of joint family for mutual aid to provide customary gifts, for the performance of ceremonies, and for retaliation (Hogbin 1934: 287). "All these ties are ties of family or kinship, and in the last resort an individual who fails to perform his obligations is penalised by the dissolution of the tie and the loss of the claims that go with it. Divorce is the commonest instance, expulsion from the joint family the extreme case" (Hogbin 1934: 388).

People banished slackers from the island. If one were ousted from kindred, then others could take vengeance because there were no relatives to assist the ousted person (Hogbin 1934: 135):

"Banishment and the loss of rights as a member of the kindred group formed a most effective penalty in a community where the support of the group was so frequently necessary." Here rights are expectations of reciprocal help from others, the basis of compliance with custom in primitive or stateless societies by Malinowski's account.

Rights are the claims that go with social relations. Without states, there is no "total community" and no claim against the totality of the community. State power can force people to do things, can deprive people of life, limb, and liberty. In addition to an ideology of the state as the source of "natural," "human," or "civil" rights, some polities develop a concept of rights as guarantees against abuses of state power, which are not problematical in nonstate societies. They therefore develop a concept of rights against the state.

In the United States, for instance: "We hold these truths to be self-evident, that all men . . . are endowed by their Creator with certain unalienable Rights, that among these are Life, Liberty and the pursuit of Happiness. That to secure these rights, Governments are instituted among Men. . . ."

The U.S. Constitution guarantees rights against the state, including "the right of the people peaceably to assemble," "the right of the people to keep and bear Arms," "the right of the people to be secure in their persons, houses, papers, and effects, against unreasonable searches and seizures," "the right to a speedy and public trial," "the right of trial by jury," and "the right of citizens of the United States to vote" irrespective of "race, color, or previous condition of servitude" or sex.

In the social democracies the notion of rights is more pragmatic—the right to employment, health care, decent housing, dignified retirement, fair remuneration, education—but it specifies what individuals may expect from the social order, identified with government.

These are quite different concepts of "right" from the legitimate expectation of others which is relevant for Nuer, Tiv, Ontong-Java, Cheyenne, medieval Iceland, or any other primitive or stateless society.

Edmond Leach (1977) argues that the capitalist societies are constructed on the assumptions that each individual is a detached unit and that all value is incorporated in material property. Therefore, "we naturally find that the sanctity of individual life and the sanctity of property are given maximum emphasis, so that it is *homicide* and *theft* which become the supreme forms of sacrilege and on that account the prototype of a public crime" (Leach 1977: 32).

Lewellyn and Hoebel (1941), Hoebel (1954), Bohannan (1957), Leach (1977), and virtually all other anthropologists who have studied primitive law warn against the transposition of the categories of the anthropologist's culture onto those of the people he or she is studying. One important thing that stateless societies share is the notion that there is no public law. It is no surprise that medieval Iceland, one among many stateless societies recorded in the ethnographic record, was similar in this respect.

William Miller (1990) argues that in medieval Iceland most rules were not intended to be absolute, but to state the usual procedure or standard practice so people did not have to negotiate every detail of every transaction. As he puts it, Icelandic law was like American commercial law.

The Icelandic word for "law" is *lög*. Here I use Richard Cleasby's (1957) spellings and definitions unless otherwise noted. It is the plural of *lag*, a stratum or layer. It means what is laid down, from the verb *að leggja*, to lay or place. *Leggja lög* is to lay down or make laws. *Leggja* has a sense of the cumulative past, of the accumulation of past events that determine the present, a sense of that which is ordained, as in *lagt er allt fyrir* "everything is laid down before" or "all is predestined." *Að leggja á*, to lay upon, means to curse, as in "I lay it on you that . . ." One can lay out expenses, words, love, hate, saddles, and nets.

*Lög* enters many combinations. *Lögrétta* was the law council (Dennis et al. 1980) or court of legislation (Miller 1990). *Rétta* means to make right or straight, to stretch out or reach out, to make right or adjust. Literally, *lögrétta* means something like law righting or repairing. It was composed of each of the chieftains and two advisors for each of them. It elected a *lögsögumaðr* (literally: law, say, man) or lawspeaker for a three-year term. He was to recite one-third of the law at each annual meeting of the General Assembly. The *lögrétta* made law, changed law, and declared what the law would be if there were disagreements. A *lögkaup* was a lawful bargain; a *löggarð* was a lawful fence; and a *löghlið* was a lawful gate. A *lögbók* was a lawbook. *Lög* attached to something else generally meant something to do with law.

The verb *að rétta* was applied when people of a district collectively drove their sheep in from the common lands in the fall to pens (*rétt*) for sorting into individual herds. *Réttr* was an adjective that meant right or lawful. The noun *réttr* meant right or law; *forn réttr*, old law; *lands réttr*, law of the land. *Réttr* meant right, due claim, atonement for injury, or the indemnity itself. It was the compensation one received for an injury. *Konungs réttr* meant the king's due.

*Að boða* means to announce or proclaim; a *boðorð* (announced word) is an order; the *Tíu* (ten) *lagaboðorð* (announced words of law) are the ten commandments. To break a commandment is *bregða*, which means to draw a weapon, to move a body part quickly, to turn or change, or to disregard or deviate from. The noun form is *afbrigð* or *afbrigði*, and a *lagaafbrigði* is a deviation from law.

Our understanding of such terms, and of the concept of law and related ideas, rests to a great extent on just how we elect to translate them. The school of translation that currently holds sway in the field of Old Norse studies advocates finding modern English analogs to Old Icelandic terms and expressions (Durrenberger and Durrenberger 1986). Thus, one might translate *lagaafbrigði* as a violation of law or a breach of law. The sense of the term, however, does not derive from "break" or "violate" but from "deviate." The metaphor of deviation is quite different in its impact and implications from the metaphor of breaking (Lakoff and Johnson 1980). The first rests on a metaphoric notion of law as a path or line from which one may deviate. The second derives its sense from a metaphor of law as a thing which can be broken or violated.

Other abstractions were metaphoric "things" which could be broken. *Að rofa* is a verb that means to break up, used of clouds, a climatic phenomenon. *Rof* is a noun that means a breach or opening. In this sense a truce (*grið*) could be broken. Failure to take an action or make a payment enjoined by a judgment (*dómr*) was judgment breaking (*dómrof*) and provided grounds for further action (Dennis et al. 1980). *Rof* also meant a reversal or retraction of a judgment and a pleader in an appeal was called a *rofsmaðr* (literally: break's-man) and such a case was called a *rofsmál* or break's-case.

In medieval Iceland, the law was a code of conduct from which people could deviate, not a thing they could break or violate. Law only takes on such thingness when it becomes the embodiment of the state in state societies. Then it defines the social order, which has objective and institutional existence in the institutions of the state. One who breaks the law violates the state itself, and the state responds with the apparatus of criminal law.

Without states there is no criminal law and law is not a thing. It defines social relations among individuals. One cannot violate the law, but one can violate individuals. *Grágás* indicates that the violation of another individual places one outside the realm of the code of conduct. One ceases to be a party to the "social contract" by one's own acts.

One of the central concepts of old Icelandic law was *helgi*, which is often translated as immunity. "Every free person not under legal penalty and everything animate or inanimate belonging to such a free person enjoyed immunity as of right" (Dennis et al. 1980: 247).

All people had *helgi* unless they lost it by their own acts, such as attacking another or being outlawed. It meant security, inviolability. The opposite of *helgi* was *óhelgi*, which was synonymous with being outlawed. While *Grágás* enjoined ordinary people to aid others under many circumstances on pain of various penalties, it specified that one could not aid those who were outlawed. Such people could be killed with impunity.

*Helgi* also meant the holy boundary of meeting within a demarcated area. The verb *að helga* meant to appropriate land; to make holy, hallow, sanctify; to prove a thing to be one's own, to make one's right to a thing good; to clear oneself of a charge; to sanctify a meeting place and fix its boundary (*þinghelgi*) (Cleasby 1957: 254–255). *Þinghelgi* was the consecrated grounds of an assembly (*þing*) or the ceremony of hallowing an assembly. Land that one claimed was sanctified in just the same sense as the person who claimed it was.

The general principle of law was that if one acted to violate another's immunity one lost one's own and therefore became vulnerable to attack. To violate another's safety was to lose one's own. *Helgi* meant consecrated, intact, inviolate, protected, pure, sacred, immune, safe, secure.

The verb *að bjarga* meant to help and the noun *björg* meant help, assistance. In *Grágás* this meant sheltering, advising, sustaining, ferrying, and sharing food and quarters (Dennis et al. 1980: 240). To so help those who were "unholy" was to forfeit one's immunity and to refuse to help others was to be liable to penalty. *Grágás* specified who was to help get a newborn baptized or help those on the way to get an infant baptized, assist travelers on the way to assemblies, aid wedding parties, and put up traders.

*Að varða* meant to warrant, guarantee, answer for. To *varða* much or little or not at all meant to matter as much, to guard or defend or warn one off from. It is the logical connection between an action and its proper consequence. *Grágás* specified that various actions warranted various responses from fines to outlawry. The general form of an entry in *Grágás* is: "It is said that something warrants outlawry, lesser outlawry, a fine of three marks."

*Grágás* specified five kinds of assaults which warrant lesser outlawry if a person inflicted one on another when they met on the way: cutting, thrusting, shooting or throwing, striking, shaking, wresting something from one's grasp, meaning to strike with a weapon, or making another fall to a knee and a hand or further.

The man who attacks a man with a legal assault will be unholy and also all those men who knew [his intentions] at the place unless the other had before been unholy by his actions.

It is also said if a man wounds a man that it warrants outlawry [forest going].

If a man kills a man, that also warrants outlawry [forest going].

The man falls unholy before him whom he has hurt and so for all the men who help him though it is right if other men avenge him if they want until it becomes another day.

It is said if a man murders a man it also warrants outlawry [forest going]. And it is murder if a man hides it or conceals the corpse or does not accept it.

*Grágás* does not specify rights, but specifies what it is to be "holy" and how one can lose that status. What a person defends is not rights but the self. What is violated is not law but the holiness of another person.

The words that mean honor derive from metaphors or words for man. *Vaskr* meant manly, valiant. *Drengr* meant rock or pillar, metaphorically an unmarried man or youth, and further, metaphorically, its usual medieval sense of a bold, valiant, worthy man. *Drengskapr* (*drengskapur*) meant temper or character of a valiant man, hence honor.

Further, concepts of honor were linked to combativeness, as among Nuer. Gunnar Hliðarendi of *Njáll's Saga*, an archetype of the sterling saga-hero, asks whether he is "a more unvaliant [*úvaskari*] man than other men because it seems to me more than to other men to fight men."

To situate these assessments in the thirteenth century, we need to appraise the practice of honor and generosity during that time. Here we can refer to the contemporary Sturlunga collection and discover thirteenth-century attitudes to *drengskapur*.

Literary performance, like humor, is intimately related to the transmission of an estimation of *drengskapur*. Einar Ól. Sveinsson paints a vivid picture of the thirteenth century drawn from the literature of the period:

> The whole country seethed and bubbled with gibing and jeering like a witches' cauldron. As soon as some noteworthy event took place, verses were made about it which in a short time spread by word of mouth from one end of the country to the other. Sometimes these verses were in the nature of chronicles and did little more than fix in meter the memory of the events, sometimes they praised the persons involved, but far more often they were in a humorous and bantering vein, or mocking and sarcastic, at times even filled with venom and gall, intended to wound and blacken and malign. (Sveinsson 1953: 91–92)

Richard Bauman (1986) points out that one way to attack someone was to attack honor through insulting verses or stories, which often evoked retaliation.

*Sturlunga Saga* indicates that the same kinds of events transpired in the thirteenth century as in the tenth and that people of the thirteenth century were keenly aware of the individuals, deeds, and events of the earlier times. There were, however, differences between the periods which help explain the preoccupations of the family sagas.

As an example of the conception of honor and everyday life as performance, Bauman cites Þórður Þorvaldsson and his brother Snorri, who, outnumbered and surrounded, determine to defend themselves rather than surrender so as to make a better story and thus enhance their honor, if not their life expectancies. This is, in fact, as good example as can be found in the *Sturlunga Saga* for the almost total absence of the substance of *drengskapur*. After some skirmishing and rock-throwing the defenders surrender to their attackers and all but Snorri give up their weapons. An attacker chops off Snorri's leg at the knee. One of the defenders says it was an unmanly stroke, but Sturla, the leader of the attackers, says it was a manly stroke. Sturla then has both brothers killed (chap. 85).

What was his motivation? While Sturla was away, the two brothers with thirteen others had attacked his house, destroyed the women's sleeping quarters, stabbed a priest who defended himself with a pillow, killed several servants, ransacked the hall, terrorized his wife, pillaged the place for everything of worth, including his weapons, cut the breasts from one woman, stole all the horses, and left as the sun came up (chap. 71).

What was Þórður's motivation for the raid? Followers of Sturla, the sons of Hrafn, had killed Þórður's and Snorri's father, Þorvaldur, by burning him in the house of a farmer he was visiting, handled their mother roughly, and stolen the weapons and horses from the farmer's house (chap. 67).

They killed Þorvaldur because he protected his brother, Bárður Snorrason, who had made the wife of the son of Jón pregnant. Snorri suggested that they would get no justice as long as Þorvaldur was alive. Contributing to Þorvaldur's bad name in Snorri's house was a man whose feet Þorvaldur had previously cut off (chap. 46).

Einar Ól. Sveinsson's assessment of such times of raid and burning, of power struggles among kin, is grimmer than Bauman's:

In the thirteenth century men have their hands so full that they cannot put the same stress on matters of form as before. They consider themselves fortunate to escape by flight, have to put up with being spoken ill of, as long as they have hopes of practical results. This does not mean that they are not touchy and sensitive of their honor, but the most pressing need must come first. The force and compulsion to which men are subjected besmirches them, they have to put up with more than before, but their sensitivity is sufficient so that malice, envy, and a tendency to criticise produce satire and slander in various forms. (Sveinsson 1953: 91)

There is still an aesthetic dimension to life, though the underlying practice of honor that informed it has changed, as we see in all of the less than honorable deeds of the voracious individuals who fought one another throughout the Sturlung period. The values of *drengskapur* are most notable by their absence in this period. It is this that makes *drengskapur* problematical to the thirteenth century and that puts it at the center of sagas of the past.

While unscrupulous and overbearing chieftains are no strangers to the family sagas, *Bandamanna Saga* puts a group of them in league together and bases its satire on their unhonorable characteristics. Sverrir Tómasson (1977) suggests the satire indicates a power struggle between rich farmers whose wealth derived from their church lands and hereditary chieftains who lacked wealth but had titles. He derives this argument from Gunnar Karlsson (1977).

While powerful farmers no doubt derived wealth from church farms, so did hereditary chieftains. Access to this source of wealth did not distinguish one from the other. In the example Karlsson cites (1977: 369) from *Svínfellinga Saga* of the Sturlung collection, the rich farmer Ögmundur is married to the aristocrat's father's sister and is foster father to and guardian of the wealth of his younger brother. Both the farmer (*bóndi*) and the aristocrat (*höfðingi*) control church farms. The aristocrat confiscates the wealth of two of the farmer's friends and visits the farmer with about eighty followers. The farmer and his men take refuge in his church; when one of their number escapes to summon help, the aristocrat, fearing the imminent arrival of superior forces, leaves. He has the farmer outlawed when no one is at the assembly to defend the farmer, thus establishing a claim to both his life and property. The chieftain allows his father's sister, the farmer's wife, to keep half of the wealth, but takes the other half, including half of the church's wealth, for himself. It is this chieftain that the farmer later kills.

The Sturlung collection is replete with examples of chieftains and other powerful figures who are more likely to take than to give, more likely to pillage than to cultivate, more likely to offer intimidation than reason or justice. There was not a struggle between poor aristocrats and rich farmers, but among equally rich and powerful chieftains, farmers, and church men.

The vision of Valhöll, Odin's hall where those slain in battle eat inexhaustible food and drink from a ceaseless flow of ale, fight daily, and repeat the feasting and fighting until the cataclysmic battle of the gods with the giants which destroys the world at *ragnarök*, is a thirteenth-century reflection of the two important dimensions of honor of thirteenth-century realities in Snorri Sturlasson's *Edda*: feasting and fighting, both manifestations of reciprocity. The principles of relevance and selection for this manual of poetry were contemporary.

The *Poetic Edda*, a collection of verses compiled by an Icelander in the last half of the thirteenth century, offers another view into the worldview of the period by indicating what its compiler(s) found valuable. Scribal errors suggest it was not written from memory or dictation, but copied from at least two manuscripts. Paleographic evidence suggests that these two source manuscripts are not older than the beginning of the thirteenth century and must have been written by different scribes. Nothing is known of its provenance or compilation or composition. Linguistic evidence suggests the verses do not predate the ninth century (Hollander 1962).

One of the verses, "The Seeress's Prophecy" details the events of *ragnarök* and "reads like the troubled vision of one rooted in the ancient traditions who is sorrowfully contemplating the demoralization of his times . . ." (Hollander 1962: xviii).

Many of the verses commemorate events among Goths and Huns of five or six centuries before, though the differences from other sources are as great as the similarities. Bertha Phillpotts notices that, while it is remarkable that any trace of events is preserved at all during this span of time, space, and culture, "there are some amazing omissions . . ." (1931: 71).

There is no mention of the Roman or Byzantine empires, though Black Sea place names occur. "There is no memory of the part played by Goths against either empire though they were at grips with them for many more centuries than with the Huns" (Phillpotts 1931: 71). While disasters are recounted, victories and conquests are not. "All their spectacular successes are forgotten— . . . these peoples remember only disaster" (Phillpotts 1931: 72).

Phillpotts's interpretation of the picture presented in the *Poetic Edda* is consistent with that derived from *Grágás*:

> The Germanic peoples never seem to have demanded that the ordering of the world should be just. With a superb arrogance, they are concerned to vindicate, not the gods, not Fate, but themselves. . . . In fact, if we are right in interpreting these ancient stories, what seemed to the Greeks Hubris, overweening pride, was to the Teutonic world the ultimate vindication of man's character and man's dignity. (Phillpotts 1931: 93–94)

In the story of *ragnarök* the gods are equal to people because, like people, their disaster is their ultimate test of character. Phillpotts argues that the verses enshrine only failure and defeat because they hold that well-met defeat magnifies a person more than any success. At *ragnarök*, "resisting to the uttermost a foreordained defeat, with the world crashing in ruins round them, the gods, as they should, outdo even their devotees. . . . They are redeemed by the final resistance, heroic because hopeless" (Phillpotts 1931: 137–138).

She contends that while the poems may not reflect history, they do represent "those moral and intellectual qualities which shape historical events."

The tendency to magnify defeat rather than success which makes itself felt in the forgetting of victory and the remembering of defeat, and in the glorification of annihilation in the *Sibyl's Vision*—surely this is the motive force behind the readiness to take gigantic risks, to face odds, to stake everything on the result of a battle, which is exemplified again and again in the history of these peoples. (Phillpotts 1931: 145)

The stanzas on fame, she suggests, represent "a challenge flung down by man to the powers ordering the world. Fate can destroy the most valiant hero, but in Fate's despite men and women can give him a life after death that is an immortality, an immortality far more precious, far more vitally interwoven into the very web and woof of Northern thought, than existence in Odin's Hall of the Slain" (1931: 128). Such an outlook informed the sense of performance that Bauman detects.

In medieval Iceland, concepts of honor followed from concepts of holiness. To respect what was holy was to be honorable. Part of that respect was to maintain one's own sense of holiness, not to allow one's self to be violated by the actions of others. That meant being ever-vigilant for any transgression and being sufficiently combative to prevent transgressions. As a general outlook, such combativeness provided pressure to settle matters peaceably rather than fight over them and contributed to the maintenance of a balance of power among individuals, a kind of universal tension punctuated by acts of violence which maintained the tension.

This balance did not last long. The political economy upon which it was predicated was transitory. The social order of medieval Iceland contained within it a dynamism that inexorably led to the strife of the thirteenth century.

During the thirteenth century, as the social and political order of stratification without a state that had been established in Iceland was in its final throes of self-destruction, Icelandic writers turned their attention to their past and wrote the Icelandic family sagas. Others wrote about contemporary events and left a record that was soon collected into the *Sturlunga* or contemporary sagas. Some writers recorded the law traditions; others wrote the sagas of the bishops. Together these writings provide a rich self-account of a stratified society without a state as it saw its own past and as it recorded its own demise (Durrenberger 1988b, 1990b).

William Miller (1990: 42) suggests that the motive for the collecting of laws was related to the impetus that produced the sagas, an anxiety to preserve something of Icelandic experience at the time it was being superseded.

When the anthropologist Roger Keesing stumbled into the midst of the Kwaio of the highlands of the Solomon Islands, he was welcomed as the fulfillment of prophecy and the answer to sacrifices. Kwaio, like medieval Icelanders, were a stateless people who had been involved on the fringes of developing empires and wars. Like medieval Icelanders, they had traveled abroad and learned alien languages and customs and brought back wealth. Like Icelanders, they had not been fast to become Christian when missionaries had been sent to them. As in Iceland, their social order was disarrayed by chaos and warfare. Like Icelanders, they wanted to record their customs and their stories. Keesing was the medium for Kwaio (Keesing 1978; Keesing and Corris 1980). At a similar historical moment, Icelanders provided their own chroniclers, whose motivations were similar to those of the Kwaio. Such motivations explain why Icelanders included sections of the law that had never been practiced, such as the complexities of the wergeld rings, with other anachronisms. By the time *Grágás* was written, about 1260, the law was less a guide to action or code of conduct than an abstraction. It simply did not matter in the face of force, which ruled the land.

It is no happenstance that we have both laws and sagas in the medieval literature of Iceland. Both are consequences of the same mode of thought centered on the concept of holiness. To respect and maintain one's holiness is to be honorable. Other works such as the *Poetic Edda* and *Snorri's Edda* derive from the same outlook and were compiled for similar reasons. Generosity and feasting as well as the artful conduct of lawsuits were paths to repute and honor. Honor, reputation, and praise are equally important for the maintenance of the value system. To enter the system, deeds have to be related as stories. Hence, sagas themselves are part of the same system as the deeds they commemorate (Bauman 1986: 146).

Far from being a document "out of time" as Kirsten Hastrup (1985) portrays it, Snorri Sturluson's *Edda* is a thirteenth-century document just as much as the family sagas, law books, and contemporary sagas are. It thus informs us about the thirteenth century. The mythical materials Snorri used were available because they reflected the same cultural postulates that informed political and social action of those times. The social reality and understandings of the myths were derivative from the same assumptions. There should be some correspondence between the myths of the *Edda* and the social reality of Snorri's time. Indeed, the Sturlung period and the *Edda* are characterized by the supposition that, while successful mediation is possible, it always results in new oppositions and that unmediated oppositions result in continued oppositions playing out in different forms and contexts. The *Edda* also reflects a contemporary appreciation of the history of Iceland. In the first stage there is creation of a new society and the specification of its structural elements. This stage is complete with the founding of the General Assembly, and the various oppositions work themselves out during subsequent episodes, but the unresolved ones grow more virulent as they repeat themselves (Durrenberger and Quinlan 1987). The only resolution Snorri could envision for his mythology was *ragnarök*, the cataclysmic final battle between the gods and the giants, between the holy and the unholy, that destroys them all.

Phillpotts (1931) concludes that the impetus for Snorri's composing his *Edda* was the imminence of the demise of the form it preserves. The Eddic poems had lost their popularity before Snorri's time or else they would not have been so corrupt and fragmentary when they were written down. Snorri was as puzzled by their language as modern readers are. Because the Norwegian kings began looking south for their models of civilization, their models of sophistication changed and skaldic verse, much of which was dedicated to the praise of kings, soon ceased to be appreciated. However, Snorri

realized that its vogue was waning. It was therefore a brilliant idea to write a guide to skaldic poetry which would necessarily also be a kind of *Who's Who* to heathen personages. . . . The skald must understand the world of ideas to which the kennings [complex but stereotyped meta-phoric references] belong,—the mythology and heroic legends of the North. (Phillpotts 1931: 231)

As the institutional balance shifts, people become more vulner-able, less inviolate, their sense of holiness is challenged by the realities of daily life in a violent and honorless period. As their sense of self is challenged, their social order collapses. Like Kwaio, they turn to their writers to record what has been in an attempt to preserve a semblance of a past order in the disorder of the present.

People of the time interpreted their experiences with the cul-tural categories they had and from their interpretations produced, among other artifacts, the family sagas and the contemporary sa-gas. In an age in which political maneuvering took precedence, people reassessed such concepts as honor, reciprocity, and law. Their valuations and revaluations informed their writing about contemporary events as well as about the past (Durrenberger and Wilcox 1990).

After 1264 when the remaining chieftain-aristocrats surren-dered their authorities to the king of Norway through Gissur Þorvaldsson, they demanded the resumption of the trade upon which their prestige so depended. Thus ended a brutal period and the nearly four hundred years of stratification without a state.

# 8. CONCLUSIONS

In 1271 the General Assemby in Iceland ratifed a lawbook named *Járnsíða* (Ironside), based on Norwegian law. Ten years later it accepted another book, *Jónsbók* (Jon's book), named for Jón Einarsson, an emissary of the king who brought the book to Iceland. It was clear that the king made the law and brooked no opposition. There were no more chieftains. The country was divided into districts to be governed by royal appointees. They judged cases and executed sentences assisted by police. There was no provision for vengeance, and criminals were seen as sinners with a right to mercy. Crimes were no longer considered violations of a person but offenses against public authority. The variety of punishments increased and included death, fines, whipping, branding, and imprisonment (Stein-Wilkeshuis 1986). Thus was the state established in Iceland.

Saga writing continued, but its subject matter changed from the Icelandic past to more fantastic venues in the vagueness of "overseas," and the events become less commonplace, more mythological or folkloric. There are warrior-princesses wooed and won by princes who perform great deeds to win them; people are transformed into animals; there are cataclysmic fights between the forces of good and evil reminiscent of *ragnarök*, the final battle between the gods and giants related in Snorri's *Edda*. Such works have been called "lying sagas" and dismissed by literary scholars as degenerate and decadent forms.

One of these is the fourteenth-century *Gautrek's Saga*, which examines different kinds of reciprocal relations and describes the possible perversions of reciprocity. There is no resolution. The shift from a system based on reciprocity to one based on principles of hierarchy, territory, and state power was fundamental.

*Gautrek's Saga* explores the theme of reciprocity in many of its possible forms, none of which was appropriate. Thus, it represents the social reality of the new state. Beyond being a decadent fantasy, this saga is a lesson in reciprocity which reflects an important issue at the time the saga was written and provides a critique of the new state order (Durrenberger 1982b).

There remains the question of what kinds of interpretations of the family sagas are warranted and how they can inform our understandings of the realities of the thirteenth century or earlier times. The same kinds of issues have been debated in the disciplines of history, literature, and anthropology (Hunt 1989).

The proper use of the Icelandic family sagas in the reconstruction of medieval Iceland's history and social order has long been contested, and the debate continues. One practice has been to compare various texts and declare unreliable those which do not match some text taken as a better representation of reality, such as the contemporary sagas or the laws.

Jenny Jochens (1980) argues that we should question the veracity of the family sagas because their accounts vary from those of law codes and the contemporary sagas. She concludes that clerics portrayed monogamy and fidelity in the family sagas as a means of promoting Christian ideals. She suggests (1986) that the strong female characters of the sagas, which she interprets as images of evil who goad men to barbarous deeds which destroy the male order of society, were created by clerical misogyny based on images of Eve, but have no counterparts in the reality of the contemporary sagas and are therefore unreal.

A second approach has been to interpret texts within a broadly comparative perspective. Carol Clover (1988) points out that the portrayals of women in the family sagas are ambivalent. She uses comparative evidence on the nature of frontier societies and those which must limit their populations to suggest the likelihood of female infanticide and of a high ratio of men to women in medieval Iceland, which, she argues, led to an overvaluation of women and the ambivalence expressed in laws and sagas. This contextualization of the texts in comparative terms obviates "the need to make a choice between right and wrong sources, it recuperates the sagas not as strictly historical sources but as realistic social documents that stand in a complementary, not contradictory, relation to the laws and [the contemporary] *Sturlunga Saga*" (Clover 1988: 182).

Clover (1985) analyzes the assumptions of saga scholarship, but leaves two unchallenged: that "artistic expression through literature" and "history" are categories which are relevant to thirteenth-century Iceland. I (Durrenberger 1985) have argued that they are not, that the debates about historicity, foreign influences, influences of other literatures, and composition are couched in modern terms which are foreign to the conceptual world of thirteenth-century Iceland. The very terms of the argument are projections of modern state-embedded assumptions about literature, society, reality, law, and stories which saga scholars have projected onto medieval Iceland.

The modern distinction between fiction and history depends on ways of distinguishing, choosing, and interpreting the materials from which to construct narratives. The sense of reality that fiction evokes is a result of "an author's ability to offer the reader a suggestive array of fictional elements that satisfy the requirements of possible reality in the shared world of writer and reader" (Partner 1986: 97). Today historians have to persuade readers that the reality is not only possible but guaranteed by specific relations to things outside the text, that the historical account mimics reality (Partner 1986: 97–98).

The problematic link in any historical or ethnographic account is the connection between narrative and reality. How can we be sure that the story we have constructed adequately represents the reality? Stories, literary or not, are indices of social meaning rather than "messages about the world" (Spiegel 1990: 61). History is ordered differently in societies with different schemes of meaning, and cultural schemes are historically ordered as people revalue meanings in their acting out of them (Biersack 1989: 86), as we have seen in medieval Iceland.

The sagas are neither art nor history, but articulations of what Claude Lévi-Strauss (1973) calls a "totemic operator," an overarching classification system which organizes all experience into an integrated whole in terms of which one can locate anyone or anything relative to all other beings, things, or forces. It defines nature, the human place in nature, and any person's place in the natural and human order. Its logic is one of classification and analogy. Genealogy functions as classification rather than as history. The concept of time is static or repetitive rather than linear and progressive. Events happen many times—are the same event— and one must only locate events within the totalizing matrix of classification of people, families, places, and things. Events are subject to the logic of classification and analogy and are treated like objects. Such conceptual systems are characteristic of "primitive," stateless societies such as medieval Iceland.

The genealogical openings and closings situate the characters in a classification system. One is one's family, and a person with no genealogy is a person with no place in the totemic system (Durrenberger, Durrenberger, and Eysteinsson 1988). If a person is a family, the family is also a place. Not only are individuals identified with families, but families, even by their physical characteristics, are identified with places. Beginning and ending with the positioning of individuals negates the sense of progressing time and brings the narration back to the beginning point. The concepts of time and genealogy are similar to Sahlins's (1981) description of such concepts in Hawaii before parallel monumental changes, "the logical means of cultural repetition" (1981: 13).

The sagamen locate the sagas in the past by showing the differences between their own time and the time of the saga and attribute the differences to events. It is the recognition of the differences that made it necessary to stitch the present to the past (Durrenberger and Durrenberger 1986; Durrenberger 1990). The sagas are time-denying artifacts, whose purpose is to stitch the realities of the thirteenth century to the cultural image of a changeless society.

The classification of events is more important than their sequence. Events are repetitive, predictable. Even if the characters try to influence future events or to act differently, the results are inevitable. What happens to a person, and what he or she does, is immanent, an aspect of the person. A person is who he or she is by virtue of the person's position in the system of classification. Thus, there is no sense of character "development." Once we know a person's characteristics and place in the classification system, we know how he or she will act. A saga character at twelve is the same at eighteen and at death.

This is part of a person's place in the scheme of things, part of his or her location in the totemic system—hence the genealogies, attention to location, and descriptions of characteristics. It is unalterable; it is laid down. Things turn out as they must. Things turn out as they will. But no person or force makes things happen according to desire or plans. Things just happen as they must, as a part of a pattern which is laid down.

The problem facing any stratified society is how to keep order and maintain privilege in the face of inequalities. The history of the Icelandic polity from the settlement to 1264 is the history of attempts to solve this fundamental problem without invoking the institutions of a state. The foundation of the General Assembly, the articulation and recitation of the law, and the accommodation to Christianity were maneuvers to keep things as they were in the face of inevitably increasing differentiations in wealth, power, and access to resources. The writing of the sagas was a similar response, an attempt to interpret contemporary events and situations of the thirteenth century in terms of an image of an unchanging society and to indicate the differences between the contemporary realities and the culturally assumed stasis. The sagas are the cultural manifestation of an effort of the same sort as the more overtly political and social developments to maintain a changeless social order in the face of change.

Within the "totemic" form there is plenty of room for authorial maneuver, just as there is within the confines of the formulae of the modern novel or drama, which demand adherence to conventions and structures that are no less restraining. Authors or composers could create characters who are the "opposites" of others along one or several dimensions of contrast. In many respects in his saga Gunnlaugur is the "opposite" of Kjartan in *Laxdæla Saga*. One can see Hrafn as the opposite of Bolli and Helga as the opposite of Guðrún. The parallels between Hallfreður in *Gunnlaugur's Saga* and Gunnlaugur are too strong to be missed. The one theme these characters are involved in also has many permutations: two men in love with the same woman, one woman in love with two men, two women in love with one man, one man in love with two women. Within this set, an author or composer could systematically alter the characteristics of each person and thus the events. The totemic outlook was at the center of saga writing as a literary tradition; *Njáll's Saga*, written late, with its artfully manipulated texture of oppositions, may be the epitome of the form.

*Hen-Þórir's Saga* illustrates the clashing of two paradigms of behavior, two sets of values, one based on social exchange, the other on monetized market exchange; in a political context of a stratified society without a state, it uses all of the devices of objective reportage to favor the former over the latter even in the face of the imminent collapse of the society it so favors. This saga reaffirms older values of chieftainship and honor (Durrenberger, Durrenberger, and Eysteinsson 1988).

Other sagas such as the saga of Hávarður and *Bandamanna Saga* portray chieftains as altogether despicable in local terms such as neglect of reciprocity, generosity, and honor and thoroughly voracious, tyrannical, and overbearing. If some sagas seem to support the ruling elite, others surely attack it with satire and wit and were forms of resistance (Durrenberger and Wilcox 1990).

Skarphéðinn, Njáll's son, is not well attested in other texts besides *Njáll's Saga* and it is quite possible that he never existed. It is feasible that Hallgerður was not as evil as the saga makes her, nor Guðrún as saintly. It is perhaps implausible, if possible, that Hávarður stayed in bed for three years, but it is even less likely that this old man made such a quick recovery from such protracted inactivity and became the terror of his enemies overnight, capable of fast pursuit, long-distance swimming, and strenuous, sustained armed combat.

But if we unravel the assumptions underlying any of these sagas, if we look for the "elements that satisfy the requirements of possible reality in the shared world of writer and reader," as Nancy Partner (1986: 97) puts it, we quickly perceive the role of Norwegian traders, sheep, hay, grass, slaves, renters, seasonal workers, chieftains, law, vengeance, honor, reputation, and combativeness. We see that there is no state, that chieftains take land when they can and want to, and that farmers and others are free to resist these transgressions. These are some of the important economic, political, sociological, and ideological dimensions of the period which the sagas reveal whether or not they are histori-cally accurate. Where there are blanks, where we do not know whether to credit the sagas, we can look at well-attested contem-porary examples of societies that are similar in criteria.

We do not need to believe that the settlers of Iceland were flee-ing from Haraldur Finehair. The important observation is that those who wrote of them said they were and gave them the mo-tivation of maintaining the sociopolitical status quo, a motive the sagamen of the thirteenth century may have projected onto their progenitors on the basis of their own experience.

One cannot look to sagas for chronology or biography or other dimensions of historical reality. These were not their nec-essary ingredients. As Knut Odner (1974: 150) observes, one can "distinguish between 'historical' and 'sociological' situations and persons, . . . the historical person Hænsa-þorir is not the same person as the Hænsa-þorir of the saga carrying his name."

Sagas are not histories any more than the novels of Jane Austen are (Handler and Segal 1985). But neither are they literature in the modern sense. In their concern with category and relation-ship, the sagas cannot avoid representing social, political, and eco-nomic reality as it was, even though details of person and time might be conflated or confused. We are therefore warranted in taking them as representations of sociological if not historical or biographical realities.

If the logic of sagas is not one of historical time, one event causing another, as in modern concepts of history, story, and the novel, but one of classification and analogy, we would expect pairs and triples, comparisons, contrasts, and the indication of similarity of classification by similarity of opposition. Things and events are organized in opposing pairs which enter into chains of analogies. It is such structures that make sagas initially unfamiliar to modern readers.

Icelanders began writing sagas about 230 years after the first "official" settler arrived around 874. Icelanders were widely trav-eled and could not have avoided contact with writing. Writing was independently invented several times to keep records of time, people, wealth, the business of all states, and then to record reli-gious and "historical" documents, also the business of states.

Nonstate peoples, on the margins of states, appropriate writing when they need to write.

When they started writing, Icelanders wrote about secular as well as religious matters. They adapted the Roman alphabet to their own tongue and wrote in the vernacular because they had something to write for one another. This process of writing started just about a hundred years after seasonal labor became available, when landowners could expand their holdings and the distribution of wealth, land, and power began to shift in a continuous process of revaluing the social and political variables.

No one knew better than the people who lived then that their stratified society without a state was unstable, because they did everything they could to stabilize it to make it conform to their ideas of a stable social order. They standardized the law and founded the General Assembly 60 years after they settled the land and, about 70 years later, even accepted Christianity to try to unify the law into a single system. After these 130 years in the land the balance was beginning to shift. It took another 120 years to reach the breakdown proportions that Morton Fried discusses (1967) and to enter the age of the Sturlungs when the sagas were written.

Looking back on these 400 years, we can see a continuous process from the first settlement to the incorporation into Norwegian hegemony. The people of the time projected what they experienced in the present onto what they knew of the past in an attempt to identify the confusions of the present with the conditions of the past, in an effort to prevent the inevitable and maintain a semblance of the social and political relations and structures of the past. Just as other totemic societies remap their social orders onto certitudes of a changeless nature, Icelanders tried to stitch the present to the past to deny the changes that permeated their lives and awarenesses. Sometimes they reflected the hegemonic values of chieftains; sometimes they resisted and mocked them.

It is no mistake that *Njáll's Saga*, a late saga, written after the decisive turning point of 1264, is so neatly structured. It is a summary of the categories and themes of the past, more or less independent of the present, which by then was unalterable even by literary struggle. The sagas ceased being written not because the form had been exhausted, or because it was impossible to follow them, or for any lack of material, but because the historical realities were now undeniable in the new system of administration and law.

The credibility of the sagas derives from their cultural function. Descriptions of events are never neutral, natural. They are always filtered through the cultural structures of the people who make them. Today we place events into historical sequences and give them relative importance on the basis of their weight in our ideology of causality. Our interpretations create the "realities." The sagas define a totemic reality which was more real to the people who created them and for whom they were created than any events or characters could have been. They inscribed aspects of their totemic system at a time when the social and political system associated with it was in the process of undeniable and important changes that affected people in their everyday lives.

If the sagas are not credible today it is because we take them as either flawed history or art, not for what they were. We cannot take them for what they were because we are all peoples of history and no longer struggle against the inevitabilities of a stateless society but accept the realities of states and their definitions of reality.

# REFERENCES CITED

Amorosi, Thomas
  1989    Contributions to the zooarchaeology of Iceland: Some pre-
          liminary notes. In *The anthropology of Iceland*, ed. E. Paul
          Durrenberger and Gísli Pálsson, pp. 203–227. Iowa City:
          University of Iowa Press.

Bauman, Richard
  1986    Performance and honor in thirteenth-century Iceland. *Jour-
          nal of American Folklore* 99: 131–150.

Becker, A. L.
  1984    Biography of a sentence: A Burmese proverb. In *Text, play,
          and story: The construction and reconstruction of self and society*,
          ed. S. Plattner and E. Bruner, pp. 135–155. 1983 Proceed-
          ings of the American Ethnological Society. Washington,
          D.C.: American Ethnological Society.

Biersack, Alletta
  1989    Local knowledge, local history: Geertz and beyond. In *The
          new cultural history*, ed. Lynn Hunt, pp. 72–96. Berkeley:
          University of California Press.

Bohannan, Paul
  1957    *Justice and judgment among the Tiv*. London: Oxford Univer-
          sity Press.
  1965    The differing realms of the law. In *The ethnography of law*,
          ed. Laura Nader, pp. 33–42. *American Anthropologist* Spe-
          cial Publication 67.
  1969    Ethnography and comparison in legal anthropology. In *Law
          in culture and society*, ed. Laura Nader, pp. 401–418. Chi-
          cago: Aldine.

Boucher, Alan, trans.
  1983    *The saga of Gunnlaug snake-tongue*. Reykjavík: Iceland Re-
          view Press.

Byock, Jesse
  1982    *Feud in the Icelandic saga*. Berkeley: University of California
          Press.
  1984    Saga form, oral prehistory, and the Icelandic social context.
          *New Literary History* 14: 153–173.
  1988    *Medieval Iceland: Society, sagas, and power*. Berkeley: Univer-
          sity of California Press.

Calder, Grace J.
  1970    Introduction. In *The story of Kormak the son of Ogmund* by
          William Morris and Eríkr Magnússon. London: William
          Morris Society.
Chayanov, A. V.
  1966    *The theory of peasant economy.* Ed. D. Thorner, B. Kerblay,
          and R. E. F. Smith. Homewood, Ill.: Richard D. Irwin.
Cleasby, Richard
  1957    *An Icelandic-English dictionary.* 2nd ed. Oxford: Clarendon
          Press.
Clover, Carol J.
  1985    Icelandic family sagas (*Íslendingasögur*). In *Old Norse-*
          *Icelandic literature: A critical guide*, ed. Carol J. Clover and
          John Lindow, pp. 239–316. Ithaca: Cornell University
          Press.
  1988    The politics of scarcity: Notes on the sex ratio in early Scan-
          dinavia. *Scandinavian Studies* 60: 147–188.
Clover, Carol J., and John Lindow
  1985    *Old Norse-Icelandic literature: A critical guide.* Ithaca: Cornell
          University Press.
Dennis, Andrew, Peter Foote, and Richard Perkins
  1980    *Laws of early Iceland.* Winnipeg: University of Manitoba
          Press.
Durrenberger, E. Paul
  1975    Understanding a misunderstanding: Thai-Lisu relations in
          northern Thailand. *Anthropological Quarterly* 48: 106–120.
  1976    The economy of a Lisu village. *American Ethnologist* 3:
          633–644.
  1979    An analysis of Shan household production decisions. *Journal*
          *of Anthropological Research* 35: 447–458.
  1980    Chayanov's economic analysis in anthropology. *Journal of*
          *Anthropological Research* 36: 133–148.
  1981    The economy of a Shan village. *Ethnos* 46: 64–79.
  1982a   An analysis of Lisu symbolism, economics, and cognition.
          *Pacific Viewpoint* 23: 127–145.
  1982b   Reciprocity in Gautrek's saga: An anthropological analysis.
          *Northern Studies* 19: 23–37.
  1984a, ed. *Chayanov, peasants, and economic anthropology.* New York:
          Academic Press.
  1984b   Introduction. In *Chayanov, peasants, and economic anthropol-*
          *ogy*, ed. E. Paul Durrenberger, pp. 1–25.
  1985    Sagas, totems, and history. *Samfélagstíðindi* 5: 51–80.
  1988a   Chiefly consumption in Commonwealth Iceland. *Northern*
          *Studies* 25: 108–120.

1988b   Stratification without a state: The collapse of the Icelandic
        Commonwealth. *Ethnos* 53: 239–265.
1989    *Lisu religion*. DeKalb: University of Northern Illinois Center
        for Southeast Asian Studies.
1990a   Production in medieval Iceland. *Acta Archaeologica* 61: 14–
        21. The Norse of the North Atlantic, ed. Gerald F. Bigelow.
1990b   Text and transactions in Commonwealth Iceland. *Ethnos* 55:
        74–91.
Durrenberger, E. Paul, and Dorothy Durrenberger
1986    Translating Gunnlaug's saga: An anthropological approach
        to literary style and cultural structures. *Translation Review*
        21–22: 11–20.
Durrenberger, E. Paul, Dorothy Durrenberger, and
Ástráður Eysteinsson
1988    Economic representation and narrative structure in *Hænsa-
        Þóris saga. Saga-Book* 22: 143–164.
Durrenberger, E. Paul, and Bob Quinlan
1987    The structure of the Prose Edda. *Scandinavian Yearbook of
        Folklore* 41: 65–76.
Durrenberger, E. Paul, and Nicola Tannenbaum
1983    A diachronic analysis of Shan cropping systems. *Ethnos* 48:
        117–194.
1992    Household economy, political economy, and ideology: Peas-
        ants and the state in southeast Asia. *American Anthropologist*
        94: 74–89.
Durrenberger, E. Paul, and Jonathan Wilcox
1990    Humor as a guide to social change: Bandamanna saga and
        heroic values. Presented at the conference From Sagas to So-
        ciety, Reykjavík.
Evans-Pritchard, Edward E.
1940    *The Nuer: A description of the modes of livelihood and political
        institutions of a Nilotic people*. Oxford: Clarendon Press.
Finsen, Vilhjálmur
1852    *Grágás*. Copenhagen: Det Nordiske Literatur Samfund.
Foote, Peter
1963    An essay on the saga of Gisli and its Icelandic background.
        In *The saga of Gisli (notes and an introductory essay by Peter
        Foote)*, tran. George Johnston, pp. 93–134. London: Dent.
Fried, Morton
1967    *The evolution of political society*. New York: Random House.
Geertz, Clifford
1973    *The interpretation of cultures*. New York: Basic Books.
1983    *Local knowledge*. New York: Basic Books.

Gelsinger, Bruce E.
1981    *Icelandic enterprise: Commerce and economy in the Middle Ages.* Columbia: University of South Carolina Press.
Gordon, E. V.
1981    *Introduction to Old Norse.* Oxford: Oxford University Press.
Gurevich, A. Ya.
1969    Space and time in the Weltmodell of the old Scandinavian peoples. *Mediaeval Scandinavia* 2: 42–53.
1971    Saga and history: The "historical conception" of Snorri Sturluson. *Mediaeval Scandinavia* 4: 42–53.
Hallberg, Peter
1974    The syncretic saga mind: A discussion of a new approach to the Icelandic sagas. *Mediaeval Scandinavia* 7: 102–117.
Halldórsson, Bragi, Jón Torfason, Sverrir Tómasson, and Örnólfur Thorsson
1987    *Íslendinga Sögur.* Reykjavík: Svart Á Hvítu.
Handler, Richard, and Daniel A. Segal
1985    Hierarchies of choice: The social construction of rank in Jane Austen. *American Ethnologist* 12: 691–706.
Hanks, Lucian
1972    *Rice and man: Agricultural ecology in southeast Asia.* Chicago: Aldine Atherton.
Hastrup, Kirsten
1985    *Culture and history in medieval Iceland.* Oxford: Clarendon Press.
Henry, Jules
1963    *Culture against man.* New York: Random House.
Hobsbawm, Eric
1983a    Inventing traditions. In *The invention of tradition,* ed. Eric Hobsbawm and Terence Ranger, pp. 1–14. Cambridge: Cambridge University Press.
1983b    Mass-producing traditions: Europe, 1870–1914. in *The invention of tradition,* ed. Eric Hobsbawm and Terence Ranger, pp. 263–307. Cambridge: Cambridge University Press.
Hodges, Richard
1989    *The Anglo-Saxon achievement: Archaeology and the beginnings of English society.* London: Duckworth.
Hoebel, E. Adamson
1954    *The law of primitive man: A study in comparative legal dynamics.* Cambridge: Harvard University Press.
Hogbin, Herbert Ian
1934    *Law and order in Polynesia: A study of primitive legal institutions.* New York: Harcourt Brace and Company.

Hollander, Lee M.
  1962    *The Poetic Edda*. Austin: University of Texas Press.
Hunt, Lynn, ed.
  1989    *The new cultural history*. Berkeley: University of California Press.
Jochens, Jenny M.
  1980    The church and sexuality in medieval Iceland. *Journal of Medieval History* 6: 377–392.
  1986    The medieval Icelandic heroine: Fact or fiction? *Viator* 17: 35–64.
Jóhannesson, Jón
  1974    *A history of the old Icelandic Commonwealth*. Trans. Haraldur Bessason. Manitoba: University of Manitoba Press.
Jóhannesson, Jón, Magnús Finnbogason, and Kristján Eldjárn
  1946    *Sturlunga saga*. Reykjavík: H. F. Leiftur.
Johnston, George
  1961    On translation-II, a comment. *Saga-Book of the Viking Society* 15: 394–402.
  1963    *The saga of Gisli (notes and an introductory essay by Peter Foote)*. London: J. M. Dent.
Jones, Gwyn
  1935    *Four Icelandic sagas*. Princeton: Princeton University Press.
Karlsson, Gunnar
  1977    Goðar and Höfðingjar in medieval Iceland. *Saga-Book* 19: 358–370.
Keesing, Roger M.
  1978    *'Elota's story: The life and times of a Solomon Islands big man*. New York: St. Martin's Press.
Keesing, Roger M., and Peter Corris
  1980    *Lightning meets the west wind: The Malaita massacre*. Melbourne: Oxford University Press.
Kottak, Conrad
  1983    *Assault on paradise: Social change in a Brazilian village*. New York: Random House.
Kuhn, Thomas
  1970    *The structure of scientific revolutions*. Chicago: University of Chicago Press.
Lakoff, George, and Mark Johnson
  1980    *Metaphors we live by*. Chicago: University of Chicago Press.
Leach, Edmond
  1977    *Custom, law, and terrorist violence*. Edinburgh: University of Edinburgh Press.

Lévi-Strauss, Claude
1963   *Structural anthropology*. New York: Basic Books.
1973   *The savage mind*. Chicago: University of Chicago Press.
Lewellyn, Karl N., and E. Adamson Hoebel
1941   *The Cheyenne way: Conflict and case law in primitive jurisprudence*. Norman: University of Oklahoma Press.
Limón, J. E., and M. J. Young
1986   Frontiers, settlements, and development in folklore studies, 1972–1985. *Annual Review of Anthropology* 15: 437–460.
McGovern, Thomas H., Gerald Bigelow, and Daniel Russell
1985   Northern islands, human error, and environmental degradation: A view of social and ecological change in the medieval north Atlantic. *Human Ecology* 16: 225–270.
McGrew, Julia H., trans.
1970a  The saga of Hvamm-Sturla. In *Sturlunga saga*, vol. 1, pp. 59–113. New York: Twayne Publishers and the American-Scandinavian Foundation.
1970b  The saga of the Icelanders. In *Sturlunga saga*, vol. 1, pp. 117–447. New York: Twayne Publishers and the American-Scandinavian Foundation.
McGrew, Julia H.
1970c  *Sturlunga saga*. Volume 1. New York: Twayne Publishers and the American-Scandinavian Foundation.
McGrew, Julia H., and R. George Thomas
1974   *Sturlunga saga*. Volume 2. New York: Twayne Publishers and the American-Scandinavian Foundation.
Magnússon, Eiríkr, and William Morris
1891   *Howard the halt*. London: Quaritch.
Magnusson, Magnus, and Herman Pálsson
1969   *Laxdaela saga*. New York: Penguin.
Malinowski, Bronislaw
1934   Introduction. In Herbert Ian Hogbin, *Law and order in Polynesia: A study of primitive legal institutions*, pp. 1–74. New York: Harcourt Brace and Company.
Marx, Karl
1977   *Capital*. Trans. Ben Fowkes. New York: Vintage Books.
Mauss, Marcel
1967   *The gift*. Trans. Ian Cunnison. New York: Norton.
Maxwell, I. R.
1961   On translation-I, a review. *Saga-Book of the Viking Society* 15: 383–393.
Miller, William Ian
1983   Justifying Skarpheðinn: Of pretext and politics in the Icelandic bloodfeud. *Scandinavian Studies* 55: 316–344.

1984    Avoiding legal judgment: The submission of disputes to arbitration in medieval Iceland. *American Journal of Legal History* 28: 95–134.

1986a   Gift, sale, payment, raid: Case studies in the negotiation and classification of exchange in medieval Iceland. *Speculum* 61: 18–50.

1986b   Review of culture and history in medieval Iceland, by Kirsten Hastrup. *Scandinavian Studies* 58: 183–186.

1990    *Bloodtaking and peacemaking: Feud, law, and society in saga Iceland*. Chicago: University of Chicago Press.

Odner, Knut

1974    Economic structures in western Norway in the early iron age. *Norwegian Archaeological Review* 7: 104–112.

Pálsson, Herman, and Paul Edwards, trans.

1973    *Eyrbyggja saga*. Toronto: University of Toronto Press.

Paredes, A., and R. Bauman, eds.

1972    *Toward new perspectives in folklore*. Austin: University of Texas Press.

Partner, Nancy F.

1986    Making up lost time: Writing on the writing of history. *Speculum* 61: 90–117.

Patterson, Lee

1987    *Negotiating the past: The historical understanding of medieval literature*. Madison: University of Wisconsin Press.

Phillpotts, Bertha Surtees

1913    *Kindred and clan in the Middle Ages and after: A study in the sociology of the Teutonic races*. Cambridge: Cambridge University Press.

1931    *Edda and saga*. London: Thornton Butterworth.

Polanyi, Karl

1944    *The great transformation*. New York: Rinehart.

Rich, George W.

1976    Changing Icelandic kinship. *Ethnology* 15: 1–20.

1989    Problems and prospects in the study of Icelandic kinship. In *The anthropology of Iceland*, ed. E. Paul Durrenberger and Gísli Pálsson, pp. 53–79. Iowa City: University of Iowa Press.

Roseberry, William

1989    *Anthropologies and histories: Essays in culture, history, and political economy*. New Brunswick: Rutgers University Press.

Sahlins, Marshall

1958    *Social stratification in Polynesia*. Seattle: University of Washington Press.

1972    *Stone age economics*. Chicago: Aldine.

1981    *Historical metaphors and mythical realities: Structure in the early history of the Sandwich Islands kingdom*. Ann Arbor: University of Michigan Press.
1985    *Islands of history*. Chicago: University of Chicago Press.

Spiegel, Gabrielle M.
1990    History, historicism, and the social logic of the text in the Middle Ages. *Speculum* 65: 59–96.

Steblin-Kamenskij, M. I.
1973    *The saga mind*. Trans. Kenneth H. Ober. Odense: Odense University Press.
1982    *Myth*. Trans. Mary P. Coote and Frederic Amory. Ann Arbor: Karoma.

Stein-Wilkeshuis, Martina
1986    Laws in medieval Iceland. *Journal of Medieval History* 12: 37–53.

Sveinsson, Einar Ól.
1953    *The age of the Sturlungs: Icelandic civilization in the thirteenth century*. Trans. Jóhann S. Hannesson. Ithaca: Cornell University Press.

Swannell, J. N.
1961    William Morris as an interpreter of Old Norse. *Saga-Book of the Viking Society* 15: 365–382.

Tannenbaum, Nicola
1984a   Chayanov and economic anthropology. In *Chayanov, peasants, and economic anthropology*, ed. E. Paul Durrenberger, pp. 27–38.
1984b   The misuse of Chayanov: "Chayanov's rule" and empiricist bias in anthropology. *American Anthropologist* 86: 927–942.

Thompson, Laura
1969    *The secret of culture: Nine community studies*. New York: Random House.

Thorsson, Örnólfur, ed.
1988    *Sturlunga saga*. Reykjavík: Svart Á Hvítu.

Tómasson, Sverrir
1977    Bandamanna saga og áheyrendur á 14. og 15 öld. *Skírnir* 151: 97–117.

Turner, Victor W.
1971    An anthropological approach to the Icelandic saga. In *The translation of culture: Essays to E. E. Evans-Pritchard*, ed. T. O. Beidelman, pp. 349–374. London: Tavistock.

Vigfússon, Guðbrandur, and F. York Powell
1905    *Origines Iclandicae*. Oxford: Clarendon.

Wax, Rosalie H.
  1969   *Magic, fate and history: The changing ethos of the Vikings.*
         Lawrence, Kansas: Coronado Press.
Williams, Raymond
  1977   *Marxism and literature.* Oxford: Oxford University Press.
Wolf, Eric R.
  1966   *Peasants.* Englewood Cliffs: Prentice-Hall.
  1982   *Europe and the people without history.* Berkeley: University of
         California Press.

# INDEX

alliances: feasts, 45
Alþing, 6, 53–55, 73; church, 76; exchange, 65. *See also* General Assembly
anthropological approach, 81
anthropologists: and Iceland, 23
Arason, Guðmundur, 71, 76–77
Arnarson, Ingólfur, 52
Arnkell, 38
Arngrímur, 72
Atli, 33
Austen, Jane, 105
authorship of sagas, 79; Sverrir Tómasson, x

*Bandamanna Saga*, 13; chieftains, 104; exchange, 67; honor, 92; reciprocity, 68–69
battle: Hafrsfjörður, 25; Órækja and Gissur, 2
Bauman, Richard: honor, 79, 91, 95
*bændur*: tax-paying farmers, 47
Bergþór: lawspeaker, 80
Bergþóra, 33
Bigelow, Gerald, 50
bishop, 6; feud arbitration, 57
bishopric, 2
Bjargey: fishing, 34
Black Sea, 94
Blund-Ketill: hay collection, 31; household, 39
Bohannan, Paul: law concepts of the Tiv, 20, 83, 86
Bolli, 12, 103
*Book of Icelanders*, 80
*Book of Settlements*, 24; force used to acquire land, 52

Börkur, 10, 11, 43
Boucher, Alan, 16
Brandur, Bishop, 76
Breiðafjörður, 43; fishing, 34
bride prices, 7
British Isles, 11, 52
Byock, Jesse, 22, 24
Byzantine Empire, 94

Chayanov, A. V., 26
Cheyenne: ideology, 79; law, 23; trouble cases, 80
chieftainship, 47, 54, 104; appropriation of land, 52; hosting feasts, 45; household economy, 29; redistributive system, 66; trading, 70–71
Christianity, 6, 75, 100, 103, 106; clergy, 17; Kwaio, 96
Christmas, 2
class, 40
Cleasley, Richard: law, 86
clothing: social status, 44–45
Clover, Carol, 22, 24; women in sagas, 100–101
coalitions, 45, 51
combativeness: honor, 90
comparative ethnography, 22
conflicts: trade, 70
consumption: driving force, 41
court system, 53–54; feud arbitration, 56
cows: household economy, 29–30
crops: grassland, 30
cultural analysis: relation to translation, 18
cultural change, 21

Denmark, 5
Dennis, Andrew, xi
dowry, 7
*drengskapur*, 79. *See also* Honor
Durrenberger, Dorothy, 15

ecological process, 39
economic choices, 29
*Edda*: honor, 93; Snorri Sturlu-
    son, 97
Edwards, Paul, 16
egalitarian society, 52
Egill, 1, 9, 11, 12, 14; conflict
    with Hermundur, 68–69
*Egill's Saga*, 4, 7, 11, 25; Skalla-
    Grímur establishes a farm, 30
Einar, 60–61; court dispute, 56–
    57; feud with Hvammur-
    Sturla, 58
Einarsson, Jón, 99
Eiríkur the Red, 11; Greenland,
    13
Eldjárn, Kristján, xi
England, 9
entourages, 51, 53, 73; chieftain's
    friendship, 45; exchange, 66;
    hierarchical relationships, 54
ethnography: comparative, 22
Evans-Pritchard, E. E.: law, 83–
    84
Eve, 100
excommunication, 76–77
execution, 53
*Eyrbyggja Saga*, 7, 10, 42; fishing,
    34; labor, 38
Eysteinsson, Ástáður: translation
    of sagas, 15

family saga: Sturlung period, x
fate, 95
farm, 5; in *Egill Saga*, 9; size, 39
feasts, 53; burdensomeness, 5;
    coalition relationships, 45;

eight days of Christmas, 2; *Gís-
    li's Saga*, 10; Hallgerður and
    Bergþóra, 33; the Lisu, 4; so-
    cial order, 14
feuds: court system, 56
fieldwork, 20–21
Finehair, Haraldur, 25, 26, 105;
    productivity, 28, 29
Finnbogason, Magnús, xi
Finsen, Vilhjálmur, xi
fish, 5, 34–35, 40
Flosi, 36, 73
Foote, Peter, 54, 56
force: and ownership, 50–51;
    power maintenance, 48
foreign goods, 36; increased need,
    46
fosterage, 72
Fried, Morton, 52, 58, 106; kin-
    ship, 78; law, 82
friendship: and trade, 70

*Gautrek's Saga*: "lying sagas,"
    99–100
Geertz, Clifford, 17, 21, 22
Gelsinger, Bruce, 36; exchange,
    65; land distribution, 32; mer-
    chants, 39, 70; production, 31
genealogy: classification, 102
General Assembly, 53–55, 57,
    80, 86–87, 99, 102, 103;
    founding, 97. *See also* Alþing
*Gift, The*, 23, 41
gift giving, 41, 51
Gísli, 9, 10, 11, 14
*Gísli's Saga*, 7, 10; feast, 45
Gordon, E. V.: honor, 77
Goths, 94
government institutions: among
    the Shan, 4
*Grágás*, 22, 29, 59, 65, 80–81,
    94, 96; law code, 55; violation
    of law, 88–90

grain, 70; brewing for feasts, 42, 45; scarcity, 46
grass, 30
Greenland, 11
Gunnlaugur, 13, 103
*Gunnlaugur's Saga*, 9, 15, 103
Gurevich, A. Ya., 23
Guttormsson, Kálfur, 63
Guðbjörg, Álf, 60–61
Guðrún, 11, 12, 13, 103, 104

Hafrsfjörður: battle, 25
Hákon, king of Norway, 2
Hálfdan, 59
Hallberg, Peter, 23
Halldórsson, Bragi: translation, x
Hallfreður, 103
Hallgerður, 8, 11–13, 33, 104; fish, 35
Hallur, 35
Hallur of Glaumbaer, 63
Hanks, Lucian, 54
Hastrup, Kirsten, ix, 55, 97; clergy, 76; *Grágás*, 81; land inheritance, 59
*Hávamál*, 23, 41
Hávarður, 34; chieftains, 104; claims new land, 32
*Hávarður's Saga*, 19, 33–34; production, 30–31
Hawaii, 102
hay: role in sagas, 30–31
Hænsa-Þórir: market economy, 68
Helga, 103
Helgafell, 11; farm, 43
Helga the fair, 9
Helgi: fosterage, 72
Hen-Þórir: entourage building, 74; socioeconomic exchange, 71–72
*Hen-Þórir's Saga*, 12; conflict between social and market ex-

change, 71, 104; grass, 31; land rental, 33; provisions, 35; social economy, 68; trade conflicts, 70
Hermundur: conflict with Egill, 68–69
heroes, 13
hierarchy: among the Lisu, 4; among the Shan, 4
historical process, 20–21
historical sources: of sagas, 21–24
Hjörleifur, 52
Hliðarendi, Gunnar, 8, 9, 13, 14, 44–45, 73; honor, 90
Hoebel, E. Adamson, 23, 80–81; law, 86
holiness: *drengskapur*, 79; honor, 95; law and the sagas, 96, 98
honor, x, 89–93, 104; *Bandamanna Saga*, 13; *drengskapur*, 79; holiness, 95
horses, 31
Höskuldur, 8, 11, 12, 14, 45
households: chieftains, 29; economy, 40; independent, 48; production of provisions, 26–27, 35; units of production, 29, 37, 38–39
Hrafn, 103; honor, 91
Hrafnkell: hirelings, 39
*Hrafnkell's Saga*: availability of land, 32; labor, 38; loss of chieftaincy, 35–36
Hrútur, 8, 11, 12, 14, 66
Huns, 94
Hvammur-Sturla, 60; feud with Einar, 58; kinship, 75
Hvítu, Svart Á, x–xi

ice age (little), 50
immunity, 88–89
inheritance, 61–62
irrigation systems, 28

jarl: title bestowed on Gissur, 2
*Járnsíða* (Ironside), 99
Jochens, Jenny: veracity of family
    sagas, 100
Jóhannesson, Jón, xi, 55
Johnston, George, 16, 19
Jones, Gwyn, 16, 55, 57
*Jónsbók*, 99

Kári, 73
Karlsson, Gunnar: ideology, 68,
    92
Keesing, Roger: Kwaio, 96
killing: *Gísli's Saga*, 10; ven-
    geance, 1, 4
King Aðalsteinn, 9
kingdom: consolidation, 25
King Eiríkur, 9
King Haraldur, 9, 11
king of Norway, 98
King Óláfur: gifts, 43
kinship, 52, 54; connections, 4;
    Ontong Java, 84–85
Kjartan, 12, 103
Kolbeinn, Tumason, 1; coercion
    to insure support, 58–59; con-
    flict with Sighvatur, 62–64; ex-
    communication, 76–77
Kolskeggur: wealth, 44
Kormákur, 13
Kveld-úlfur, 9
Kwaio, 96, 98

labor, 6
laborers, 38; production, 32
land: acquisition, 52; distribu-
    tion, 6
landless class, 48–49
landowners, 15, 47; Haraldur, 26
law, 14, 59, 81; church, 76; de-
    viation, 88; state institutions, x;
    Tiv, 20
law council: *lögrétta*, 86
lawspeakers, 53, 55, 86

*Laxdæla Saga*, 7, 11, 12, 14, 43,
    103; fish, 34; wealth, 44
Leach, Edmond: law, 82–83,
    85–86
Leifur: Vínland, 13
Lévi-Strauss, Claude, 23; totemic
    operator, 101
Lewellyn, Karl, 23, 80–81; law,
    86
Lindow, John, 24
Lisu, of Thailand, 3; ideology, 79;
    religion, 17–18
literary criticism, 16
livestock, 6, 30–31
Loftsson, Jón, 61
love: Kormákur and Gunnlaugur,
    13
luxury goods, 49
"lying sagas," 99

McGovern, Thomas, 50; ecologi-
    cal process, 39
McGrew, Julia: translation, xi
Magnússon, Eiríkr, 16; and Mor-
    ris, 19
Magnusson, Magnus, 16; and
    Pálsson, 19
Malinowski, Bronislaw: law, 81–
    82; reciprocity, 84–85
market economy, 35, 49; rela-
    tions, 65
market system, 15
Markússon, Jón, 63
marriage, 53
Marx, Karl: consumption, 42
Másson, Hafliði, 80
Mauss, Marcel, 23, 41
Mead, Margaret, 20
merchants: no class development,
    39
Miller, William: ideology, 81; kill-
    ing as a political act, 45; law,
    86; saga production, 96
misogyny, 100

Morgan, L. H., 23
Morris, William, 16, 19
Mörður, 8; entourage, 45; exchange, 73

negotiation: exchange rates, 65
Ndembu, 3
Njáll, 8, 14, 66, 73
Njáll's Saga, 3, 7, 11, 12, 14, 73; feast, 45; fish, 35; honor, 90; labor transactions, 32–33; social wealth, 36; totemic outlooks, 104; trade and usury, 66; wealth, 44
nonmarket economy, 67, 73
Norse: settlements, ix; settlers, 5
Norway, ix; hegemony, 106; trade, 5, 46, 49, 66
Nuer: combativeness, 90; ideology, 79; law, 83–84

Oddur, 68–69; wealth, 67
Odner, Knut, 23, 24; historical accuracy of the sagas, 105
Ófeigur: exchange, 67–68
Óláfur, 11, 12
Ontong Java: obligation, 84–85
oral tradition, 22
Orkneys, 70
Órækja, 1, 63, 75; pillaging, 60
Ósk, 63
Ósvífur, 11, 12, 43
outlawry, 89
ownership, 73; by force, 50–51

Pálsson, Herman, 16, 19
Partner, Nancy: historical accuracy of the sagas, 104
pattern: in sagas, 14
Patterson, Lee, 21
Phillpotts, Bertha, 94; Snorri's Edda, 97
pillage, 93
Poetic Edda, 93–94, 96

police, 99
political economy, 80; Hen-Þórir's Saga, 12
political organization: change in household economy, 28
political rhetoric, 29
Polynesia: internal redistribution system, 37
Powell, F. York, 16, 19
productivity, 27–28
property, 7; among the Lisu, 4; among the Shan, 4
provisions, 32–33
public law, 86

Radcliffe-Brown, A. R.: law, 82
reciprocity, x, 84; exchange, 40, 66; nonmarket economy, 67; perversion of, 99; relationships, 36; social order, 14; trade, 70
reconciliation: Órækja and Gissur, 2
redistribution system, 37, 66
religion: of Lisu, 17–18
rent, 7; farmers to chieftains, 48; land, 33
reputation, x
resources, x
revenge: Egill on the sea, 9
Rich, George, 23
rights, 85
Roman alphabet, 106
Roman Empire, 94
Roseberry, William, 21
ruling class, 59
Russell, Daniel, 50

Saga of Guðmundur dýri: trading status of chieftains, 71
Saga of Hvammur-Sturla, 58; court disputes, 56
Saga of the Icelanders, 3, 42, 58, 59–62, 66–67, 70; excommunication, 76–77

*Saga of Þórður kakali,* 63
Sahlins, Marshall, 21, 22, 69; Hawaii, 102; internal redistribution system, 37
satire: *Bandamanna Saga,* 13
seasonal labor, 7, 33, 46, 50
settlement: of Iceland, 5
Shan, of lowland Thailand, 4
sheep, 31, 36
Sighvatsson, Sturla: property, 59
Sighvatur: conflict with Kolbeinn, 62–63; kinship, 78
Sigríður, 60
Skálholt, 2
Skalla-Grímur (Grim the bald), 5, 9, 40; establishment of farm, 30; household unit, 37, 39
Skarphéðinn, 104
slavery, 6–7, 47, 73; Irish, 52; *Laxdæla Saga,* 11; production, 32
*Snorri's Edda,* 96, 99
Snæfellsnes peninsula: settled by Norse chieftains, 11
social: agency, 21; losses, 35; maneuvering, 74; order, 14; organization and change in household economy, 28; political maneuvering, 39–40; relations as basis of economy, 14, 73–74; stratification, 53, 58
Solomon Islands: Kwaio, 96
sorcerers, 3, 10, 18
Spiegel, Gabrielle, 21; social agency in sagas, x
spirits, 4, 18
state, 7; society, 20; society and law, 82; system, 15, 51
Steblin-Kamenskij, M. I., 23
Steinar, 30
Steinarsson, Birningur, 60–61
Steinþor, 34
stinginess, 69

stratified society, ix, 53, 58, 74, 96, 103, 106; state system, 51
Sturla, 1, 3; court dispute, 56–57
Sturlunga period, x, 2, 48; escalation of warfare, 5
*Sturlunga Saga,* 3, 14–15, 95; believability, 22; court disputes, 56; honor, 91; kinship and church, 75
Sturluson, Snorri, 1–3, 10–12, 38, 42, 43, 70–71; appearance trick, 46; court disputes, 56; death of, 1; *Edda,* 97; honor, 91–93; inheritance, 62; kinship, 75, 78; lawspeaker, 55
subsistence goods, 42
Sveinsson, Einar Ól., 66; chiefly arrogance, 61; kinship and church, 75; literary performance, 90; power struggle among kin, 92
*Svínfellinga Saga,* 92

tables of equivalent values, 65
taxes, 6
tax-paying farmers, 47
Thai: entourage, 54; lowlanders, 3
Thailand: exchange, 72
Thomas, R. George: translation, xi
Thompson, Laura, 23
Thorsson, Örnólfur: translation, x–xi
timber: consumed by chieftains, 46
time: in sagas, 102
tithe law, 6, 75–76
Tiv: law concepts, 20, 83
Torfason, Jón: translation, x
totemic: outlook, 104; system, 101–103
Tómasson, Sverrir: authorship of

sagas, x; exchange, 67; ideology, 92; reciprocity, 68–69
trade, 35; Iceland, 5; Norway, 66, 69
translation, 15–19, 20; of law, 86–87
Turner, Victor, 3, 24

Úlfar, 38
unification: of Iceland, 2
United States Constitution, 85
Unnur the deep-minded, 11
usury, 66

Valgarður the gray, 45
Valhöll: honor, 93
vengeance: enforce laws, 7; of Njáll, 8
Vésteinn, 10, 14
Víga-Glúmur's Saga: hay, 30
Vigfússon, Guðbrandur, 16, 19

Wax, Rosalie, 3, 23
wealth: accumulation, 66; social stratagems, 36, 49; support, 72
Wilcox, Jonathan: translation, x
Williams, Raymond, 20
women: in sagas, 100
wood: housebuilding, 42
wool, 39–40, 42, 70; exchange with Norway, 36, 46

worldview: of sagamen, 18
writing: origins, 105–106

Þorbjörn, 33–34
Þorbrandssons, 38
Þorbrandur: labor, 38
Þórdís, 10
Þorgeir, Helga, 60
Þorgerður, 9, 11, 12
Þorgilsson, Ari, 80
Þorgrímsson, Önundur, 63
Þorgrímur, 10, 11, 14
Þórir, 13
Þórkell, 10, 43; building a church, 44; feast, 45
Þorleifsson, Dugfus, 60
Þorleikur, 12, 60
Þorsteinn: pasture defense, 30
Þóroddur: fish, 34
Þórólfur, 5, 34, 38
Þorvaldsson, Gissur, 1, 2, 5, 42, 60; kinship, 78; Norway, 98; trade, 51
Þorvaldsson, Þórður: honor, 91
Þorvaldur, 72; fish, 35; honor, 91–92
Þórður, 1, 3; conflict with Kolbeinn, 63–64

Ögmundur: honor, 92
Örlygur, 38